Fall and Winter Gardening: 25 Organic Vegetables to Plant and Grow for Late Season Food

Fall and Winter Gardening: 25 Organic Vegetables to Plant and Grow for Late Season Food

By R.J. Ruppenthal, Attorney/Professor/Garden Writer

Chapter 1: Introduction: Late Season Gardening

When springtime comes, there's a natural impulse to plant. The warm weather and longer days of summer provide the perfect combination to ripen all those tomatoes, peppers, cucumbers, green beans, squash, and melons. With the bountiful harvest in and the late summer heat beginning to fade, it seems like a good time to dig up the garden, not start a new one. But with a little planning and care, fall can be a great time to grow vegetables and extend the bounty all year long.

This book describes 25 varieties of vegetables you can plant late and grow deep into the year for harvest in late fall, winter, and early spring. All the vegetables covered here are hardy in cool temperatures. They will thrive in cool fall weather and they can handle an early frost. Some of them can handle a hard frost and keep on trucking, particularly when they are protected using one of the techniques covered in this book.

Many of these vegetables can be stored during the winter and kept until you need them. A few of them can even be left in the ground and covered with a thick mulch blanket over the winter for the first harvest of the new year in early spring. All of them are delicious and can be eaten fresh or preserved by freezing, drying, canning, or pickling them for later use.

There are other cool season veggies that I have not included in this book. Brussels sprouts, parsnips, rutabagas, leeks, and garlic, for example, can grow well in the cool fall weather. I have left them out of this guide because they need to be in the ground for much of the year in order to produce a good crop. But you just picked your tomatoes and you don't have six months to wait until the weather turns cold. Instead, I have chosen to focus on 25 vegetables that can be planted and harvested relatively quickly in just 20-75 days from planting to harvest. These are the crops that not only can be harvested late, but planted late as well.

Chapter 2: 25 Vegetables for Cool Seasons

Here are basic descriptions and planting directions for 25 cold weather vegetables. All of them are vigorous plants that grow well from seed. There is some variation in the information provided for each one. For example, larger types of broccoli may need more space to grow than smaller varieties. And the "Days to Maturity" figure is somewhat approximate, particularly since fall weather can be cool and vegetables can take a bit longer to mature.

Before proceeding, I must pay respects to the plant known as *Brassica oleracea*. This remarkable species provides us with a wide range of hardy cultivars: broccoli, cauliflower, kale, cabbage, collards, and kohlrabi. Even radishes, turnips, arugula, cress, and the Asian greens on this list are all closely related. Everything in this family is extremely nutritious to eat and tough enough to survive the cool weather of fall.

These brassicas (or cole crops, as they are often known), are the foundation of cold weather gardening. But don't worry, this book will teach you how to grow potatoes, carrots, lettuce, beets, and many more vegetables beyond the brassicas. They will be some old favorites and a few vegetables you've probably never heard of or tasted!

Descriptions of the 25 vegetables are below. But first, here is a quick rundown on the format for each description. For each vegetable, I have included the following information as well as some specific growing tips and other relevant advice.

Name of Vegetable

Edible Portion: Describes which parts of the plant may be eaten.

Days to Maturity: Gives you the expected number of days from seeding or transplant to harvest. There are two caveats here: First, some seed growers use this number to refer to "days from seeding to harvest" but most use it to mean "days from transplant to harvest". This difference is significant, especially in the fall garden, where a few days can have a huge impact. Please assume that this number refers to "days from transplant to harvest". If you are direct seeding, you will need to add some extra time to account for how long it takes the seeds to germinate and grow into seedlings fit for transplanting. Second, as I explain in an upcoming chapter, plants grow more slowly in cool fall weather than they do in the spring and summer. So just to keep our planning conservative, a little more time will be added to account for this.

Spacing: How far apart should you space seedlings? And if you are growing them in rows, how far apart should the rows be spaced? These numbers are geared towards traditional row culture, but if you are gardening in raised beds or containers, you can squeeze the spacing a bit tighter. If you are planting seeds in the garden directly, a common practice is to plant more than you need and thin them (by pinching off the extra plants you do not need or pulling them up if this does not damage the remaining plants' roots). Unless thinning is mentioned in the plant descriptions that follow, please assume that each spacing suggestion describes proper spacing between thinned plants, not seeds. Feel free to plant seeds closer together and thin them to the spacing recommendation. We normally thin plants when their first true leaves (after the seed leaves) appear. By this time, we can judge which plants are healthiest and should remain, removing the others.

Planting: How deep should you plant the seeds? For the plants on our list, this ranges from 1/4 inch to one inch deep. For the ones that need 1/4 inch to 1/2 inch planting depth, I often do not plant them at all. I just scatter them and then cover them with a thin layer of soil or compost, followed by a good watering.

Temperature for Seed Germination: What are the minimum and optimum temperatures for this plant's seeds to germinate? This information is approximate, but it will give you a good idea of the range from cold to ideal. So if you want to direct seed your crops in cool weather, you know about how cold they can handle and still sprout up from seed. And you also know at what temperature they are happiest to sprout up. They normally germinate more quickly at this warmer temperature than at the minimum temperature, which is why late summer is a great time to plant a late season garden.

Germination Time: After planting seeds, how long can you expect to wait before seeing the little plants emerge from the soil? This is important because some of them are pretty long in cool weather, and you do not want to be waiting 21 days for germination if you are already cutting things close with the frost dates. If it's already cool outside and you need to get the seeds going more quickly, bring the little pots indoors, where room temperature is usually quite close to their optimum germination temperatures.

Transplant Seedlings at: This number is very approximate. I have tried to provide an expectation of how long to keep your seedlings in little pots before planting them out in the garden. There are some standard estimates available for each of these vegetables, but most of them are inaccurate because they are geared towards spring planting. Plants that are started from seed in late summer will enjoy warmer temperatures than in the springtime. They will grow more quickly at the beginning, though once the weather cools down, they'll grow more slowly than spring crops. This means that you can plant out those fall seedlings a little sooner. The estimates for each vegetable are based on my research, but they are estimates only. Plant your seedlings a little earlier or later if you want.

And here are the descriptions for the 25 vegetables on our cool season list.

Arugula (Roquette)

- Edible Portion: Leafy greens
- Days to Maturity: 35 for baby leaves, 45-50 for larger leaves
- Spacing: Space seeds 4-6 inches apart in rows 6 inches apart
- Planting: Plant seeds ¼ inch deep
- Temperature for Seed Germination: 40 F (min.), 67 F (ideal)
- Germination Time: 5-7 days
- Transplant Seedlings at: 2-4 weeks

Arugula is a vigorous plant with green leaves that carry a sharp, peppery flavor. It has been a favorite at many gourmet restaurants. Young leaves are somewhat mild and can be eaten raw in salads. They are commonly used in salad mixes to provide an element of spice. Larger leaves are spicier and need to be cooked, which removes much of the sharp flavor. Those who enjoy the taste of arugula can use it as a spinach substitute in any recipe. Arugula is a great source of vitamins A and C as well as iron. Here is a picture.

Arugula (Roquette)

Beets and Chard

- Edible Portion: Roots (beets), leafy greens (chard)
- Days to Maturity: 55 for tender beets, 50-60 for chard leaves
- Spacing: Space seeds 4 inches apart for baby beets, 6 inches apart for larger beets, in rows 12-18 inches apart
- Planting: Plant seeds 1/2- 3/4 inch deep. When plants emerge, thin to strongest plant per cluster.
- Temperature for Seed Germination: 55 F (min.), 86 F (ideal)
- Germination Time: 7-14 days
- Transplant Seedlings at: 3-4 weeks

Both beets and chard come from the same species of plant, *Beta vulgaris*. While beets have been bred into a subspecies to maximize their root size, chard is used for its leaves and stems. Beets are sweet, earthy, and high in antioxidants. They are grown for sugar production in some parts of the world. Beets can be eaten raw in salads, roasted, or added to soups for a brilliant purple base. Chard can be used like spinach and added to soups, casseroles, pastas, rice dishes, and more. Beet greens can be cooked and eaten like chard. Each beet or chard seed actually is a cluster of seeds, so several little plants will emerge from the same location. Once they have two real leaves, choose the strongest plant and thin out the others. You can do this by pinching off the others or by pulling them out if this can be done without damaging the roots of the remaining plant.

Bok Choy (Pac Choi)

- Edible Portion: Leaves and stems
- Days to Maturity: 45-50
- Spacing: Space plants one inch apart in rows 18 inches apart.
- Planting: Plant seeds 1/4 inch deep.
- Temperature for Seed Germination: 45 F (min.), 75 F (ideal)
- Germination Time: 7-12 days
- Transplant Seedlings at: 2-3 weeks

Bok Choy is the classic stir fry vegetable in Chinese cooking. It usually has tender green leaves and succulent white stems, though some varieties have green stems (Ching-Chiang) or purple leaves (Violetta, Red Choi). Bok choy can be used as a substitute for cabbage or spinach in many recipes. Tender young leaves are good in salads as well. Like most Asian greens in the cabbage family, bok choy will bolt and go to seed very quickly in warm weather, but fall is an ideal time to grow it.

Broccoli and Cauliflower

- Edible Portion: Florets, top parts of the stems, and leaves
- Days to Maturity: 60-70 (broccoli), 60-80 (cauliflower)
- Spacing: For broccoli, space plants 12-18 inches apart, in rows 24 inches apart. For cauliflower, which is larger, space plants 18-24 inches apart in rows 24-30 inches apart.
- Planting: Plant seeds 1/4-1/2 inch deep.
- Temperature for Seed Germination: 50 F (min.), 75 F (ideal)
- Germination Time: 5-10 days
- Transplant Seedlings at: 3-5 weeks

Broccoli and cauliflower are two of the most popular vegetables on our cool season list. You can eat them raw with dips, steam them, stir fry them, cook them in casseroles, blanche them for salads, and much more. Both plants are quite easy to grow and tend to be successful fall crops, which is not always the case with them in the spring. As day lengths shorten and temperatures begin to drop, the plants are much less likely to bolt. They are more likely to reward you with a mature head of florets for fresh eating. Most growers like to keep cauliflower heads white, which you can do by tying the leaves over the heads as soon as these heads reach 1-2 inches in width.

To prolong your broccoli harvest and increase its quantity, you can plant a "sprouting broccoli" variety. When you cut off the main head, it will produce more florets from side shoots, providing you with quite a bit more broccoli. Sprouting varieties to look for include Santee and Apollo (be sure not to confuse them with seeds used for "broccoli sprouts", like the alfalfa sprouts used for sandwiches). Here is a picture of some purple broccoli below. Various types of broccoli and cauliflower produce heads in white, light green, dark green, orange, and purple hues.

Cabbage

- Edible Portion: Leaves and stems
- Days to Maturity: 60-90
- Spacing: Space plants 12 inches apart in rows 24-36 inches apart.
- Planting: Plant seeds 1/2 inch deep.
- Temperature for Seed Germination: 45 F (min.), 75 F (ideal)
- Germination Time: 5-10 days
- Transplant Seedlings at: 3-5 weeks

Cabbage, which grows in a great diversity of sizes, colors, and shapes, is one of the most popular vegetables. Cabbage makes a great addition to soups, casseroles, and other dishes. It can be chopped or shredded and eaten raw in salads. Its leaves can be steamed and used as wraps for rice and meat dishes. European style heading cabbages are the foundation for sauerkraut, while the Korean dish kimchi uses Napa cabbage as its base ingredient. Both of these fermented foods were developed as ways to preserve fresh cabbage and its valuable vitamin C over the winter months. Some cabbage heads store well over the winter as well.

Cabbage is extremely hardy and can handle both heavy frosts and snows, which only seem to improve the flavor. Large, heading varieties of cabbage take longer to mature than loose leaf cabbages. You can plant them as early as June and watch them head up into giant beach balls for fall harvest. If you plan to harvest the leaves at a younger stage before the plant heads up, then you can space plants closer together and pick them earlier.

Carrots

- Edible Portion: Roots
- Days to Maturity: 65-80 (earlier for baby carrots)
- Spacing: Space seeds one inch apart. If you plan on large carrots, you can thin them to two inches apart.
- Planting: Plant seeds 1/4 inch deep.
- Temperature for Seed Germination: 46 F (min.), 75 F (ideal)
- Germination Time: 10-21 days (at longer end of the range in colder soil)
- Direct seed only

Sweet, full flavored homegrown carrots are no match for anything you have ever bought from the store. I have never even tasted carrots from a farmers market or fruit stand that compares with what we have grown at home. Carrots are rich in beta carotene, which produces vitamin A, and they provide lots of important minerals and fiber. They taste delicious raw, either plain, in salads, or dipped in hummus or ranch dip. You can juice them, roast them, steam them, or cut them into soups, stir fries, beans, or pasta dishes. Kids love picking and eating them.

Carrots do not transplant well, so you must plant seeds directly into the garden. This is one of my regular crops, which I sow at intervals throughout the growing season. I do not follow any conventional planting directions. Because the seeds are so small, I just scatter them on top of the soil, cover it with ¼ inch of compost, water well, and then thin out any plants that come up too close together (keeping the plants 1-2 inches apart).

Like most plants on our cool season list, carrots grow fine in containers. Here are some fall carrots harvested from an Earthbox container in our garden. The beans and cherry tomato were the last blasts from some summer plants that had frozen back. My kids picked these carrots and washed them. I held them back from eating these just long enough to snap a picture.

Cauliflower: please see "Broccoli and Cauliflower"

Chard: please see "Beets and Chard"

Chicory/Endive

- Edible Portion: Leaves, stems
- Days to Maturity: 45-65
- Spacing: Space chicory 2-3 inches apart, in rows 18 inches apart
- Planting: Plant seeds 1/4 inch-1/2 inch deep.
- Temperature for Seed Germination: 50 F (min.), 75 F (ideal)
- Germination Time: 7-21 days
- Transplant Seedlings at: 3-5 weeks

Chicory is a group of vegetables that includes some gourmet members: endive, escarole, frisee, and radicchio. Chicory, not lettuce, is the most widely used base for salads in Italy, and other European countries are not far behind in terms of its popularity. There is quite a bit of diversity in this family, from the tight heading red radicchio common in Italy to the blanched Belgian endive to the spiky leaved, mild flavored frisee favored by French chefs. Chicories are not all that popular in the United States and even major seed catalogs sell very few kinds. The best seed selection, and a good source of education on chicories, can be found at Johnny's Selected Seeds.

Collards and Kale

- Edible Portion: Whole plant, minus the roots
- Days to Maturity: 60-80
- Spacing: Space plants 18 inches apart, in rows 18-30 inches apart
- Planting: Plant seeds 1/4 inch-1/2 inch deep.
- Temperature for Seed Germination: 45 F (min.), 75 F (ideal)
- Germination Time: 5-10 days
- Transplant Seedlings at: 4-6 weeks

Collards and kale are in the same family as cabbage, broccoli, cauliflower, kohlrabi, and many of the Asian greens. Both are at the top of the vegetable nutrition charts, packing whopping amounts of vitamins, minerals, and antioxidants into each serving. Collard greens are a traditional favorite in the southern United States, often fried in oil or lard with onions or bacon added. Kale, which makes great soups, is one of the most winter hardy vegetables which only seems to sweeten after a good frost. The names of kale varieties like Red Russian, Siberian, and Winterbor attest to its hardiness.

Proper spacing depends on how big you want to let your plants get; the leaves can be harvested young or you can let the plants grow large enough to take over several square feet in the garden. Begin by spacing plants 6 inches apart, in rows 18-30 inches apart, until baby leaves can be picked at around 30 days. Then begin harvesting whole plants to give the remaining plants 18 inches of spacing between plants to grow larger.

One way or another, I usually end up with a lot more kale than my family will eat by the end of the year, which I usually harvest and juice. I then freeze the dark, nutrient rich juice into ice cube trays and pop these ingots of condensed nutrition into freezer proof containers. Each time we cook something like beans, pasta, or pizza, I shave in a little frozen kale juice that is rarely noticed. What the kids don't know won't hurt them (and, in fact, should make them stronger). Entire ice cubes can be hidden in some soups.

Kale: Please see "Collards and Kale"

Kohlrabi

- Edible Portion: Bulbs (enlarged stems)
- Days to Maturity: 40-80
- Spacing: Space plants 4-5 inches apart, in rows 24 inches apart
- Planting: Plant seeds 1/4 inch-1/2 inch deep.
- Temperature for Seed Germination: 45 F (min.), 75 F (ideal)
- Germination Time: 5-17 days
- Transplant Seedlings at: 4-6 weeks

Though kohlrabi is in the same brassica family as many plants on our list, it provides a nice change of pace from all the leafy greens. Kohlrabi forms an edible swollen stem just above ground that is sweet, flavorful, and delicious. These spiked balls look like something from another planet. Though it is not a root vegetable, the taste and texture are perhaps most similar to a mild and tender Daikon Radish. Kohlrabi tastes great in stir fries and can be used like a root vegetable in soups and stews. But it really excels as a raw vegetable when eaten plain or with a dip. Pick it when it is small, with a bulb no wider than 2 inches, for best flavor. Larger bulbs with their tops removed can be kept in storage over the winter to provide 2-3 months of fresh eating. Superschmeltz is the largest storage variety, producing 8-10 inch wide bulbs. The picture below shows green and purple kohlrabi bulbs.

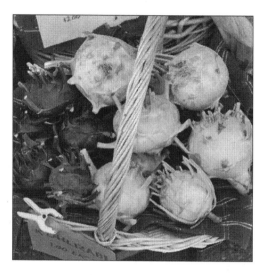

Lettuce

- Edible Portion: Leaves and stems
- Days to Maturity: 40 (baby leaf lettuce), 50-65 (full sized heads)
- Spacing: For baby leaf harvest, sowing seeds one inch apart is adequate in rows 18 inches apart. For full sized lettuce, space plants 8-10 inches apart (leaf types) or 12 inches apart (heading types).
- Planting: Plant seeds 1/4 inch deep or sow them and cover with a thin layer of soil or compost
- Temperature for Seed Germination: 40 F (min.), 60 F (ideal)
- Germination Time: 2-14 days (longest in cool weather)
- Transplant Seedlings at: 3-5 weeks

Lettuce is the essential base for our favorite salads. It comes in many more shapes and sizes than what you see in the grocery store. There are Crisphead, Butterhead, Looseleaf, Romaine (Cos), and Batavian lettuces with many varieties in each of these groups. You can pick baby leaf lettuce in just over a month from planting or grow it to full size and harvest full sized heads for a big salad from each one. If growing leaf lettuce to a large size, you can keep harvesting individual leaves on a "cut and come again" basis. To do this, use a sharp knife and cut the leaves about two inches above the base. The plants will have enough energy to keep growing and producing more leaves, which can continue for quite awhile in cool weather.

Whatever kind you grow and however you choose to grow it, lettuce is a good candidate for multiple plantings throughout the growing season. I make a small planting of new lettuce (enough for a few salads) as often as every 2-3 weeks from early spring into winter. If some of it is lost during a heat wave in August or a killing frost in December, I have only lost a few plants and I just keep planting more. We generally have more than we can eat, which we feed to the chickens in our backyard. With all that vitamin A, they make great fresh eggs with deep golden yolks.

As with some of the other vegetables on this list, you can have the best of both worlds with baby leaf lettuce and full sized lettuce. Just plant the seeds at one inch intervals and then start thinning them into your salad when they get to an edible size. If you like microgreens, you could start thinning in the first few days, but otherwise, you could wait until the plants have a few true leaves. Keep thinning until you get to the recommended spacing intervals for full sized leaf lettuce (8-10 inches apart) or head lettuce (12 inches apart), leaving one plant in each interval to mature.

Mache (Vit)

- Edible Portion: Leaves and stems
- Days to Maturity: 50
- Spacing: Mache is a very small plant. You are fairly safe just scattering the seed on a bed and covering it with ½ inch of soil or compost. Alternatively, you can space seeds an inch apart in rows 8 inches apart.
- Planting: Plant seeds 1/2 inch deep.
- Temperature for Seed Germination: 41 F (min.), 60 F (ideal)
- Germination Time: 10-15 days
- Transplant Seedlings at: 4-5 weeks

This mild little vegetable is known by several names: mache, vit, corn salad, and lamb's lettuce. The flavor is very mild, slightly nutty, and pleasing. Mache is one of the most widely consumed greens in Britain, Germany, Spain, and France, and it has become naturalized as a weed in many European gardens. This may be the origin of the name "corn salad" which probably came about because the plant grew in the field between the stalks of corn.

The mache plant grows small leaves in a rosette. Once it reaches 2-3 inches in height, it is ready to harvest, and you can use a knife to cut it off at the root. The whole plant can be used raw in salads or cooked like spinach. It is high in vitamins A, B6, and C, contains lots of omega-3 fatty acids, and provides more iron than spinach. Here is a picture of a mache plant growing.

Miners Lettuce (Claytonia)

- Edible Portion: Leaves, stems, and flowers
- Days to Maturity: 40
- Spacing: Plant 6 inches apart, in rows 12 inches apart
- Planting: Plant seeds 1/4 inch deep.
- Temperature for Seed Germination: 45 F (min.), 60 F (ideal)
- Germination Time: 2-15 days
- Transplant Seedlings at: 3-4 weeks

Miners Lettuce is extremely cold tolerant. In most of the United States, it can grow through the winter in unheated greenhouses, growing tunnels, or cold frames. The plant has attractive heart or disk shaped leaves on a long stem. As the plant grows, a small flower stalk emerges from the center of each leaf pair. You can eat it all: leaf, stem, and flower. The plant is high in vitamin C, omega-3 fatty acids, minerals, and antioxidants.

As the name indicates, this plant grows wild in many places. One of those places is my backyard, where I never planted it. Each year, a patch of Miners Lettuce comes up in the back corner. We eat a few salads' worth and then I let the rest of it grow, carefully collecting the seeds and scattering them around the back lawn. Each year, there are a few more plants and the patch spreads. To me, this is a much better way to use the yard than having a grassy lawn. I only wish it grew for more than a few months each year because I love having it for salads. Maybe I'll have to plant some of those seeds in my garden beds.

Orach (Mountain Spinach)

- Edible Portion: Leaves
- Days to Maturity: 45
- Spacing: Plant one inch apart, thinning to 6 inch spacing, in rows 12-18 inches apart
- Planting: Plant seeds 1/4 inch-1/2 inch deep.

- Temperature for Seed Germination: 45 F (min.), 60 F (ideal)
- Germination Time: 7-15 days
- Direct seed only

Orach is an underappreciated vegetable in the spinach family, which also is related to wild lambsquarters. It bears some similarities to spinach with its arrow shaped leaves and their savoyed curls. But its palette of colors is quite unique, ranging from emerald green to deep purple to bright magenta. Orach makes a great addition to mixed salads and can be cooked like spinach as well.

If you decide to plant Orach, just seed it directly in the garden, as it does not transplant well. There is good news and bad news regarding the seeds. Unfortunately, Orach seeds can be hard to find and they are expensive, since this plant is not widely grown in the United States. Look for the purple and magenta leaved types, which produce vibrant colors that look great in salad mixes. On the plus side, you will not need to spend more money on Orach seed. This must be one of the most prolific seed producing plants in the vegetable garden and the seeds stay on the plant for easy picking. You can save all you want for your next planting and still have a lot left to give away. Here is a picture of some orach plants.

Parsley

- Edible Portion: Leaves and stems. Hamburg parsley produces an edible root.
- Days to Maturity: 75-80
- Spacing: Space peas at least 6-8 inches apart in rows 12 inches apart.
- Planting: Plant seeds ½ inch deep
- Temperature for Seed Germination: 45 F (min.), 75 F (ideal)
- Germination Time: 10-21 days
- Transplant Seedlings at: 4-6 weeks

Parsley is a green, leafy plant in the carrot family. Both curly leaved and flat leaved (Italian) varieties are grown commonly in home gardens. The plant is biennial, meaning that it grows on a two year life cycle. Therefore, even if its leaves die back, it may come up again the next spring, but it will be looking to flower and seed pretty quickly the second time around. Most people grow parsley as an annual and just remove the plant when it is finished for the year.

Parsley has a mild flavor that most people like. It is quite nutritious, packing large amounts of vitamin A and K, folate, iron, and calcium. While parsley is grown as an herb in the west, people in the Middle East use parsley more like a vegetable. Tabbouleh is a bulgur wheat salad, but the grain is not the main ingredient: chopped, flat-leaf parsley has the starring role, supported by chopped mint, tomatoes, green onion, and perhaps cucumber and other vegetables. The dressing is heavy on the lemon juice and salt for a wonderfully sour, salty, mildly minty, and definitely parsley-ey taste. A good tabbouleh will help you believe that parsley should be classified as a vegetable, not an herb. Also, look for Hamburg parsley, which produces an edible root like a carrot.

Peas

- Edible Portion: Seeds, seed pods, shoots
- Days to Maturity: 10 for shoots, 60 for pods and small peas
- Spacing: Space peas at least one inch apart in rows 12-18 inches apart.
- Planting: Plant seeds ½ inch-1 inch deep.
- Temperature for Seed Germination: 40 F (min.), 80 F (ideal)
- Germination Time: 9-36 days (at longer end of the range in colder soil)
- Direct seed only

Peas are a close relative of beans. Beans are easily divided into two groups: pole beans and bush beans. For some reason, no one uses these same designations with peas, even though there are taller and shorter varieties of them also. Instead, peas usually are divided into shell peas (where you eat only the seeds), snap peas (where the whole pod is sweet, tender, and edible), and snow peas (with an edible pod that is flatter and not as sweet, commonly used in Asian stir fry dishes). Here is a picture of some Sugar Sprint peas growing in my garden in front of some Rouge d'Hiver Lettuce.

Many modern varieties grow on dwarf vines that reach only 2-3 feet in height. These are the kinds you want for fall gardening, because they are faster to mature than the ones that reach 4-5 feet tall or higher. Tall varieties also need to be staked or trellised, whereas most types of snap peas remain under 30 inches and do not need support. I recommend the following varieties for fall gardening, which are all short vined and offer quick harvests. *Sugar Snap Peas*: Sugar Snap, Sugar Ann, Sugar Sprint, Cascadia. *Shelling Peas*: Green Arrow, Maestro, and Dakota. *Snow Peas*: Dwarf Grey Sugar (best variety for edible shoots), Mammoth Melting, Oregon Sugar Pod.

Potatoes

- Edible Portion: Tubers
- Days to Maturity: 60-80 (early types), 80-100 (midseason types), 100+ (late types)
- Spacing: Space seed potatoes 12 inches apart, in rows 30 inches apart
- Planting: Plant seeds 6-9 inches deep
- Temperature for Seed Germination: 40 F (min.), 65 F (ideal) for sprouting
- Germination Time: Immediate, when seed potatoes are sprouting
- Plant seed potatoes directly; do not transplant

Potatoes are classified here as a vegetable, but their carbohydrates make them more of a grain substitute and food staple. They can be roasted, fried, mashed, steamed, boiled, baked, and prepared in numerous ways. Most potatoes are classified as baking or boiling types. Baking potatoes are starchy and floury; they also lend themselves well to mashing or frying. Good baking types include Goldrush, Red Pontiac, All Blue, and the Russet types. Boiling potatoes, such as Red Norland, Yellow Finn, and the fingerling types, are waxier and have a higher moisture content. Boilers are better for roasting, barbecuing, or boiling for potato salad.

Though potato seeds exist, it is much more efficient to plant seed potatoes, which are either small potatoes or chunks of larger ones. Each seed potato needs to have at least one "eye" which will sprout into the potato's growing shoot. You can sprout potatoes you buy from the store or order certified disease free seed potatoes from a reputable supplier, which will give you access to early, mid season, and late maturing varieties, including many delicious varieties you have never tasted before. My favorite places to buy seed potatoes are Irish Eyes Garden Seeds, Potato Garden, and Fedco Seeds' Moose Tubers.

Planting them 6-9 inches deep is about right. Potato production increases if you "hill" the potatoes. When the leaves emerge from the ground and their stems are 6-8 inches high, mound up some soil or mulch around the base of the plant to cover part of the stems (but not the leaves). When the potato stems grow out again, mound up some more soil. You can do this several times and the potato plants will root from the buried stems, producing more tubers from those roots.

Potatoes grow extremely well in containers, including large pots, tubs, and barrels. I highly recommend trying fabric pots or growing bags, which I have found to be the most successful for spuds. These cloth or plastic containers have small holes on the sides and bottom of the container, which prunes the roots and forces them to branch out, again creating more space for spud production. They also keep the soil in a good temperature range, which is warmed by the dark colored container material, yet kept from overheating by the aeration on the sides. I challenge anyone to grow a greater quantity of spuds in the equivalent amount of space in a regular garden row or even a raised bed. I do not think the productivity of fabric pots and growing bags can be beat, except by an extreme vertical growing method. For more in-depth information on these methods, and on growing spuds in general, please see my e-book entitled *How to Grow Potatoes: Planting and Harvesting Organic Food From Your Patio, Rooftop, Balcony, or Backyard Garden*, which is available in both Kindle and print editions on Amazon.

Radishes

- Edible Portion: Roots, leafy greens
- Days to Maturity: 21-30 days
- Spacing: Space seeds 1-2 inches apart, in rows 12-18 inches apart
- Planting: Plant seeds 1/2 inch deep.
- Temperature for Seed Germination: 45 F (min.),
- Germination Time: 4-10 days
- Direct seed only

Radishes often win the prize for the earliest finishers. In cool, spring weather when summer crops cannot be planted yet, home gardeners across the country are picking their first radishes. They can be grown in the fall, too, even in short season climates. There are many different kinds of radishes from the small Cherry Belle and French Breakfast radishes to the giant white daikons which add a mild sweetness in Asian cooking.

The leaves are pretty rough, but are quite edible once they're boiled. They taste great in soups. Follow spacing instructions above for small, salad-type radishes. For longer radishes and daikon, follow planting directions on seed packet label. Radishes make great pickles and fermented dishes. Here is a picture of some different kinds, including the pink-hearted Watermelon Radish, being pickled in a jar.

Scallions (Green Onions)

- Edible Portion: Immature bulb and stalk
- Days to Maturity: 60-65 days
- Spacing: Space seeds 1/4 inch-1/2 inch apart, in rows 18 inches apart
- Planting: Plant seeds 1/2 inch deep.
- Temperature for Seed Germination: 45 F (min.), 70 F (ideal)
- Germination Time: 6-12 days
- Transplant Seedlings at: 4-8 weeks

Scallions, also known as green onions or bunching onions, are immature onion plants that are picked and eaten before they can create a bulb. Scallions can be chopped and cooked like onions in almost any dish. They can be eaten raw if you like their zesty flavor, which is a little stronger than chives. They make a great accent in salads or as a topping for baked potatoes.

Bulbing onions take many months to grow, but you can harvest scallions within two months of first sowing. While scallions are just onion plants picked early, there are several varieties which have been developed specifically for this stage of harvest. Most seed suppliers sell seeds for bunching onions, while some of the better nurseries also carry onion starts or seedlings that you can transplant into your garden. Evergreen and Parade are two commonly sold varieties that grow straight as an arrow, while Guardsman and Purplette may taper to a small bulb.

Spinach

- Edible Portion: Leaves and stems
- Days to Maturity: 40-50 days

- Spacing: Space seeds 1-2 inches apart for baby leaf spinach or 3-5 inches apart for larger leafed plants, in rows 14-18 inches apart
- Planting: Plant seeds 1/2 inch deep.
- Temperature for Seed Germination: 40 F (min.), 75 F (ideal)
- Germination Time: 5-12 days (at longer end of the range in colder soil)

Spinach is the default leafy green vegetable for cooking. The young leaves can be eaten raw and make a delicious salad base. And of course spinach can be cooked in every kind of dish from eggs to lasagna. Spinach is extremely nutritious, providing large amounts of vitamin A, vitamin C, folate, iron, zinc, and other minerals with each serving. As Popeye the Sailor Man said, "I'm strong to the finish when I eats me spinach." Fortunately, you won't need to eat it from a can, and the homegrown kind is much better tasting.

Spinach plants, like the other leafy greens on this list, thrive in cold weather. It is one of the fastest fall vegetables you can grow, bringing you a harvest of baby greens in just over five weeks. The plants can be spaced very close together if you are growing them for baby greens.

Some varieties of spinach are better suited to spring production than fall production, so it is worth buying the right kind of seed. Seedlings sold in nurseries are not necessarily the best kind, and often they are simply labeled as "Spinach" with no variety listed. Bloomsdale, an old heirloom variety with, is the standard fall favorite. Also look for Giant Winter Spinach, Dolce Vita, Renegade, and Samish. Like Bloomsdale, the savoyed (curly) leaf types tend to perform the best in cold weather.

Tatsoi

- Edible Portion: Leaves and stems
- Days to Maturity: 45-50 (earlier for baby greens)
- Spacing: Space plants one inch apart in rows 18 inches apart.
- Planting: Plant seeds 1/4 inch deep.
- Temperature for Seed Germination: 45 F (min.), 75 F (ideal)
- Germination Time: 5-15 days
- Transplant Seedlings at: 2-3 weeks

Tatsoi is an Asian green with a savoyed, spinach like leaf. The small leaves grow in a very attractive, multilayered rosette. They can be picked at any stage and always stay very mild and tender. Tatsoi leaves are great in salads and they can be cooked as a substitute for spinach in any kind of dish.

Turnips

- Edible Portion: Roots, leaves
- Days to Maturity: 45-65 days
- Spacing: Space seeds 1-2 inches apart, in rows 12-18 inches apart
- Planting: Plant seeds 1/4 inch-1/2 inch deep.

- Temperature for Seed Germination: 40 F (min.), 75 F (ideal)
- Germination Time: 5-10 days
- Direct seed only

Turnips are dome shaped root vegetables that provide a great flavor to cooked dishes. In particular, they taste great when roasted, mashed and seasoned like potatoes, or added to soups. While they resemble potatoes when cooked, they have many fewer calories and also provide plenty of vitamin B6, vitamin C, potassium, and calcium. Turnip greens can be cooked as well, adding a strong dose of vitamin A and additional minerals.

Turnip roots should be picked when small and tender (no wider than three inches), as they are much tastier at this age. However, if you are planning to store cut roots over the winter, then larger ones probably store well with their tougher skins and lower moisture content. The standard turnip variety that is grown most often is called Purple Top White Globe, while Golden Globe (or Golden Ball) is also common. Some newer varieties of turnip that are picked small and eaten raw like radishes include Scarlet Queen, Scarlet Ohno, and White Egg. Occasionally, you will see leafy varieties of turnip being marketed by seed suppliers as forage food for livestock. Here is a picture of the standard Purple Top White Globe kind.

Watercress (Upland Cress)

- Edible Portion: Leaves, stems
- Days to Maturity: 45-65 days
- Spacing: Space plants 6 inches between plants, in rows 12-18 inches apart.
- Planting: Plant seeds 1/4 inch deep.
- Temperature for Seed Germination: 45 F (min.), 65 F (ideal)
- Germination Time: 3-10 days
- Transplant Seedlings at: 2-3 weeks

Watercress is a challenge to grow in the home garden, but Upland Cress provides a very similar leaf and flavor. It is also very easy to grow and was used for providing winter vitamin C in colonial times. Upland Cress has a sharp, spicy flavor that can liven up a late season salad. These plants are very hardy and can survive some ugly frosts. In all but the coldest climates, they should keep on growing right through the winter.

Be careful about leaving it too long, though, because this cress can naturalize and do a pretty good impression of weed. I planted some Upland Cress which escaped my raised beds and took over a patch of the walkway. When planting, you can sow the seeds one inch apart in row and begin thinning out the extra plants into your salads 10 days after plants emerge. Eventually, six inch spacing is best. Always give Upland Cress plenty of water, though it is not an aquatic plant like its better known relative.

Chapter 3: Starting Vegetables from Seed

There are three ways to start plants for your garden. The first way is to plant seeds directly into the garden soil, whether this is in a container, raised bed, or garden row. The second way is to start the seeds in small nursery pots and then transplant the seedlings into their eventual garden home. And the third way is to purchase seedlings at a nursery that you can plant. For various reasons, the first two approaches are best.

Direct seeding is much easier to do in the later summer than in the early spring, when most seeds are sown. In the springtime, the temperatures are still cool and variable, whereas most fall and winter crops are planted in more favorable weather. Late summer warmth helps seeds germinate quickly and gets plants off to a good start before the weather begins to cool. Also, there is a far better selection of cool weather vegetables available from seeds than from seedlings. A good seed supplier may carry as many as ten varieties of broccoli, while you would be lucky to find one variety of broccoli seedling at your local nursery. You may be missing out on some faster, more productive, tastier, disease resistant, and unusual varieties.

Growing your own seedlings and then transplanting them into the garden is a good option also. This approach still saves you money over buying seedlings, and it gives you the great selection of seeds. Growing your own seedlings is as easy as buying the seeds and planting them in small plastic pots. Once your seedlings get big enough, you can transplant them into the garden. You do not need grow lights, heat mats, or indoor greenhouses to start these seeds. Just grow them outside, since late summer has plenty of light and heat to get these plants off to a good start.

As a practical matter, very few nurseries offer a good selection of veggies for late season planting. Once the crowds of tomato planters have moved through, the nurseries tend to focus on other lines of business besides seedlings. At best, you may find a few broccoli, cabbage, and lettuce seedlings. Some of these may have been sitting on the shelf for long enough that their roots are tangled and their leaves are yellowed. If your nursery carries a better selection than this and brings in fresh stock of fall vegetable seedlings every few days, then you should be thankful because it is one of the few.

Transplanting does not work well for orach, peas, potatoes, carrots, radishes, or turnips (which prefer to be planted directly in the garden), but using this method for other vegetables on our list can save you some very valuable time. If you have limited growing space and are not ready to take out your summer tomatoes to make room for fall vegetables, then this can buy you a few extra days as well. Of course, both direct garden seedling and growing seedlings requires that you have access to high quality seeds.

I have purchased seeds from a lot of different sources in the past. Most of them sell you smaller packets of what has been left over from their larger commercial suppliers. I have bought seeds before that were old, unable to germinate, or even mislabeled as a different variety (which you find you the hard way much later). On the opposite extreme are a few great seed companies which reliably offer fresh seed that germinates quickly and grows strong plants that comply perfectly with their catalog and website descriptions. Here is a list of the best seed companies I have found. Without recommendations from people I trust, I will not buy seeds from anywhere else.

If you have a newer version of Kindle or are reading this on your computer or in the online Cloud Reader, you should be able to click these companies' names to be linked to their sites. If you are using an earlier Kindle reader, then you can find these same websites listed in the Resources section at the end of this book.

1. **Johnny's Selected Seeds**. Johnny's is the gold standard for garden seeds and offers the best selection of fall vegetables. When you browse the listings for carrots, spinach, broccoli, or other veggies on our list, you will see that Johnny's often recommends certain varieties for spring and others for late season planting. Their folks work diligently to research and test the best varieties of vegetables, particularly those that succeed in cold climates and offer good disease resistance. Every seed packet I have ordered from Johnny's has contained the absolute highest quality seeds. If you live in the Northeast, mid-Atlantic, or Upper Midwest, these seeds will be particularly well suited to your regions. I do not live in any of those regions, yet this is still my first stop. http://www.johnnyseeds.com

2. **Territorial Seed Company**. Territorial is another terrific seed supplier which puts a lot of effort into developing and testing the best varieties. I have never gone wrong ordering from them. They have an excellent selection of fall vegetables as well, though not quite as extensive as Johnny's. Territorial's seeds are particularly well suited for anyone on the West Coast. http://www.territorialseed.com

3. **Park Seed**. Park Seed also offers very reliable seeds of high quality which have tested well in their own gardens. This is an ideal seed source for southern gardeners, many of whom can grow vegetables right through the winter with little or no frost protection. http://parkseed.com

4. **High Mowing Organic Seeds**. This small Vermont company has built a successful business by growing and selling only organic seeds. They may not have as many choices as larger seed houses, but they also do not stick to the safe, popular mainstream varieties. They pick the best ones which are most likely to succeed and give you some great food. I have come to trust both their quality and their selection of varieties in each category. And I love supporting an all organic small business. http://www.highmowingseeds.com

5. **Peaceful Valley Farm and Garden Supply**. Peaceful Valley may be an unusual choice to appear on this list because it is not really a seed house. As its name indicates, this is a supply

store for farmers and gardeners. I include it here because these folks also sell seeds and I have had good success with them. If you happen to need some supplies (anything from tools to fertilizers to organic insect control to chicken coops), they throw in free seed packs when you buy enough other stuff. You get to choose a certain number of free seed packets when you buy $50, $100, etc., worth of other products. So if you need to equip your garden, you can get free seeds. http://www.groworganic.com

At most times of the year, it takes only a week or two for your seeds to ship out. Seeds are normally packed fresh after the previous year's growing season, so most people order them in the wintertime or early spring for spring planting. For fall planting, you can order seeds in the springtime and summer also, but beware that popular varieties can sell out by then. I usually order them by early spring (if I remember) and keep the fall seeds in a cool, dark cabinet until I'm ready to use them.

Once you get your seeds and your garden is ready for them, follow directions on the packet for planting. Proper planting depth, plant spacing, growing tips, and estimated times for germination, transplanting, and harvest for cool season vegetables are covered in the previous chapter. If you are planting seeds in small pots to be transplanted later, try 3-4 inch plastic nursery pots. You can grow them outside, but make sure you keep them well watered as small pots can dry out quickly in summer heat. During hot spells or in very warm climates, you may want to place the seedling pots in an area that gets some afternoon shade.

Chapter 4: When to Plant in Your Area

Most crops for fall and winter harvests should be planted between June and September. Your best planting date will depend on two variables: what you're planting and when the weather gets really cold in your area. Fast crops like radishes and baby leaf lettuce can be harvested just a few short weeks after seeding, which means you can plant them quite late. On the other hand, carrots require at least two months to grow, so you need to plan well and put them in the ground in late summer.

Every plant we cover here is pretty hardy and can handle a light frost. But young, tender plants cannot stand up to extreme cold. You need to give them a head start so they can get big enough before frost is expected to arrive. Once you know when frost is expected to arrive, you can count backwards the number of days it takes to grow a particular vegetable. That provides you with the safest planting date.

The information in the following sections will help you determine when to plant particular vegetables for the latest possible harvest in your particular area. Please bear with me, since there is a lot of information to cover first, but I think it is worth spending the proper time to understand this well. This knowledge will empower you to plan your late season garden. And I promise you we will put all this information together very soon and help you find the best planting times. Of course, it all depends on what veggies you want to grow and when your area gets frosty...

Growing Times for Vegetables

The two charts below show the estimated days to maturity for each vegetable covered here. The numbers show the amount of time it takes from planting until the earliest expected harvest date (excluding immature stages, such as baby leaf lettuce). During cool weather, plants will require more time to grow than this, so to account for this and play it safe, **please add three weeks (21 days) to each number below**. The numbers in these charts should give you a starting point to begin your planning. (The same information is included within the descriptions of each vegetable in Chapter 2).

Days to Maturity (Chart 1)

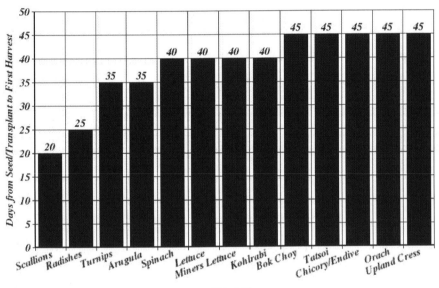

Days to Maturity (Chart 2)

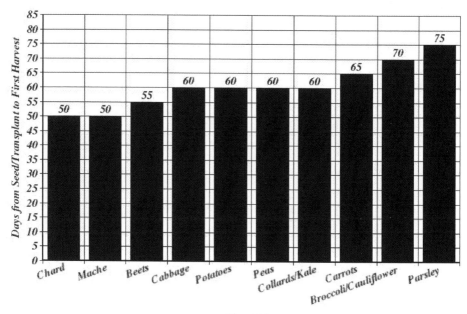

Chart showing Days from Seed/Transplant to First Harvest for various vegetables:
- Chard: 50
- Mache: 50
- Beets: 55
- Cabbage: 60
- Potatoes: 60
- Peas: 60
- Collards/Kale: 60
- Carrots: 65
- Broccoli/Cauliflower: 70
- Parsley: 75

Y-axis: Days from Seed/Transplant to First Harvest
X-axis: Vegetables

Organic veggies, including purple kohlrabi, scallions, beets, oriental greens, and arugula

Finding Your Frost Date

To find the last possible planting date for a particular crop in your climate, you can begin by finding your first average frost date in the fall (not to be confused with your last average frost date, which occurs in the spring). Knowing your first average frost date will help you determine how late you can plant and grow vegetables in your area. The list below shows you the first average frost dates for each state's capital city. If you want to find a more specific listing for the city closest to you, the Victory Seeds website has a more comprehensive geographic listing at http://www.victoryseeds.com/frost. If you live outside the United States, check with the agriculture department in your province or administrative region.

Frost dates can vary widely in large or geographically diverse states. For example, Florida's capital city (Tallahassee) has a first average frost date of 10/28, while its largest city (Miami) has no frost. First frost dates in Nevada range from August to November. And these will always be approximate, because even local microclimates have a great deal of variation. The temperature can vary by as much as 10 degrees from a hilltop to a valley bottom. As a result, these dates merely provide a place to start, and from there you will need to relay on your own observations.

Here are the first average frost dates for the capital cities of each state, plus the District of Columbia.

Alabama: 10/29
Alaska: 9/5
Arizona: 11/18
Arkansas: 10/27
California: 11/14
Colorado: 9/20
Connecticut: 9/23
Delaware: 10/21
District of Columbia: 10/23
Florida: 10/28
Georgia: 10/25
Hawaii: none
Idaho: 9/22
Illinois: 10/6
Indiana: 10/7
Iowa: 9/21
Kansas: 10/1
Kentucky: 10/10
Louisiana: 11/4
Maine: 9/22
Maryland: 10/11
Massachusetts: 10/5
Michigan 9/18
Minnesota: 9/21
Mississippi: 10/14
Missouri: 10/1

Montana: 9/2
Nebraska: 9/30
Nevada: 9/2
New Hampshire: 9/8
New Jersey: 10/23
New Mexico: 9/30
New York: 9/19
North Carolina: 10/21
North Dakota: 9/7
Ohio: 10/3
Oklahoma: 10/21
Oregon: 9/28
Pennsylvania: 10/4
Rhode Island: 9/17
South Carolina: 10/21
Tennessee: 10/14
Texas: 11/5
Utah: 9/29
Vermont: 9/8
Virginia: 10/13
Washington: 9/30
West Virginia: 10/5
Wisconsin: 9/25
Wyoming: 9/9

Once you start growing in the fall and begin to take note of the first frost date, you might realize that it often seems inaccurate. You may go through three years where the actual first frost occurs weeks later than this prediction, which may give you false confidence that you can push things further into the fall. The next year, frost comes 10 days before the average date and kills all the young plants in your garden. Remember, the date is an average, not a guarantee. And local climate conditions often move in cycles, with a few warm years followed by some really cold ones.

Killing Frosts

For most gardeners, the frost you really need to worry more about is the first hard frost or "killing frost". This is when the mercury falls to 28 degrees (F) or below, killing leafy growth on even some of the hardiest vegetables. The U.S. Climatic Data Center (http://www.ncdc.noaa.gov) provides a helpful tool for judging the probability of when the first hard frost will arrive in your area. This data is not as easy to interpret as a simple frost date, but it provides 10%, 50%, and 90% likelihoods on a particular date of the temperature reaching 28, 32, and 36 F degrees. This is especially useful for the hard frost (28 F) figures, which are not commonly available elsewhere.

Also, when reviewing this information, bear in mind that frost can occur in your garden even when recorded temperatures stay in the high 30's F. This is because weather stations record the temperatures five feet above the ground, while cold air sinks to ground level and this is where your plants grow. There is an official weather recording station two blocks from my home which never records the same temperatures as I see in my yard. It is always a few degrees higher from my thermometers (and I've tried several, just to be sure). With that much local variation possible, you can use the official numbers as a starting point, but be ready to keep an eye on the garden yourself. If a killing frost seems possible in your garden based on the weather forecast, then it may be time to harvest, unless you want to eat frozen vegetables tomorrow morning.

If you need more information about local frost or growing conditions, it is best to check with an expert in your area. The people who know it best are your county's Master Gardeners and agricultural extension agent, who have public duties to share information with local gardeners. Also, a high quality local nursery or a knowledgeable local farmer can be great sources of information as well.

Here is how I analyze the Climatic Data Center information to help determine planting times. First, the 10% and 90% levels are helpful to see, but I use the 50% level as my benchmark. Then I look at both the 32 F and 28 F dates to get a ballpark idea of when these frosts might occur. I plan to harvest (or am ready to harvest if the need arises) a few days early, just to be on the safe side.

Notice that, for various locations across the United States, the time gap between the expected first light frost (32 F) and the first hard frost (28 F) usually falls in the 9-21 day range. For example, Denver has a separation of 11 days, Boston has 14, Dallas has 15, and Atlanta and Sacramento both have 20. Assuming our plants are big enough by then, they should survive a light frost and hopefully be able to grow for a few more days. We should harvest them before the hard frost comes unless we want to take our chances.

Putting It All Together: Three Possible Planting Strategies

By now, you may be thoroughly confused and wondering why I still have not given you a planting date. What should we do with all this information and how does it help us? Gardeners take different approaches to selecting a good planting date for late season gardens. Let's put all this information together and look at three different approaches to selecting a good planting date.

Approach #1 (Coldest Areas, Most Conservative)

This approach uses the first average frost date as a harvest date. It is the most conservative strategy, since you are taking on less risk of a killing frost (28 F degrees) by being ready to harvest at the expected arrival of the first light frost (32 F degrees). This approach also makes the most sense in colder areas where there are only a few days of separation between the expected light and heavy frost dates. Here is how it works.

Step 1: Choose a vegetable you want to grow and find its estimated days to maturity. Let's use Kohlrabi as an example, which needs 40 days to mature from planting to harvest...in warm weather. But remember that earlier in this chapter, I recommended adding 21 days to this date to account for cooler fall weather when plants grow more slowly.

40 + 21 = 61 growing days needed.

Step 2: Find your first average frost date and count backwards for the required number of growing days. Let's take Springfield, Illinois, which has a first average frost date of October 6. Counting backwards 61 days, that gives us a planting date on or about August 6. Using this approach, August 6 would be the best planting date for kohlrabi in Springfield, Illinois. Of course, you could plant it earlier, but your kohlrabi would not last as late into the year in storage. From an October 6 harvest, since kohlrabi with its top cut off will last in storage for 2-3 months, you are ensuring yourself some fresh vegetables into December and possibly January. Of course, you could pickle it, dry it, or (ironically) freeze it for extended enjoyment.

Approach #2 (Mild Winter Areas, Somewhat Riskier)

This second approach counts backward from the anticipated date of the first hard frost, not the first light frost. The idea is that all of the plants on our list are hardy enough to survive a light frost, but the hard frost will kill or severely damage most of them. Therefore, why not give your plants a few extra days or weeks of growing time, harvesting them just before hard frost?

Obviously, this approach carries added risk. An average date has as many occurrences before it as after it, so you have a good chance of losing your whole crop in any given year that you push things this late. But if you watch the forecast carefully and stand ready to pick everything if frost seems imminent, then you can take advantage of these few added days of growing weather.

Be mindful, also, that you are not just selecting a harvest date, but a planting date also. This means that your vegetables may not have matured if you need to pick them early. In most cases, this is not a problem, since new potatoes, baby leaf lettuce, and baby carrots are delicacies that command even higher prices in stores. But if your cabbage hasn't headed up yet or your broccoli florets are still small, then just remember they would have been ready, had you planted them just a little sooner.

Step 1: To calculate a planting date using this approach, you use the Climatic Data Center information to find the date when there is a 50% chance of temperatures dropping to 28 F degrees. (Actually, the report says "below" 28 F degrees, but I will continue to ignore this, since it makes the calculation more difficult and this is such an inexact science to begin with). This time, let's use Chattanooga, Tennessee as an example and try to squeeze some extra growing days beyond the first 32F degree frost (November 4) and first 28 F degree hard frost (November 16).

Step 2: Choose your vegetable, find the days to maturity, and count backwards from the first hard frost date. Let's try potatoes this time; the early maturing varieties require 60 days. Potatoes are a good candidate for pushing the season, since it is possible to harvest them before maturity at a slightly smaller size. Remember to add 21 days for the cooler temperatures and slower growth.

60 + 21 days = 81 growing days needed (but a little less is OK for potatoes).

Find November 16 on the calendar and count backwards. That should put us in the ballpark of August 28. This is the last ditch planting date for potatoes in Chattanooga, Tennessee under this second approach.

Approach #3: Rolling Harvest (Hedging Your Bets)

The third approach allows you to hedge your bets by planting portions of yo9ur crop at different times. This aims for a rolling harvest where your plants will mature a week or two apart. You will be virtually assured of harvesting some veggies without frost damage, while later plantings will run that risk. You never sacrifice your whole crop, only parts of it. There are two different ways to plan for this.

Option #1: Starting in the summertime (no later than the planting date identified in Approach #1 above), plant a few vegetable seeds every week (not stopping before the planting date identified in Approach #2 above, and perhaps continuing even after that). This creates a rolling harvest, where you'll have a few more plants to pick each week or so into the fall. You may lose the later plantings, but the earlier planted veggies will have been picked by the time the hard frost hits.

Option #2: Divide your full planting into two, three or four portions, and stagger these plantings by a few days each. Again, you can use the dates in Approach #1 and Approach #2 as first and last sowing dates. If you prefer, you could plant the first portion earlier or the last one later. This way, you will be almost assured of harvesting 25-50% of your crop with the rest of it pushing Mother Nature's envelope a bit deeper.

Why Push It?

After reading the last section, you may wonder why gardeners would bother pushing their harvests by a few extra days (of cool, slow growth weather). Doing so involves a greater risk of frost damage. I think there is a pretty good argument for using Approach #1 and avoiding such a risk. However, there are some good reasons for growing later into the fall, besides the obvious reason of trying to get bigger veggies in those last few days.

One reason is that potential storage crops like potatoes, turnips, carrots, kohlrabi, and cabbage have limited storage lives. The later you can pick them, the deeper into the winter they can last. If you can prolong their time in the ground by two weeks, then that is two more weeks they could last before the potatoes start sprouting and the carrots start bending without breaking.

A second reason is that mature crops store better than those picked early. A mature potato has a tougher skin and lower moisture content than a potato which was picked early. The tougher skin and lower moisture content can prolong its storage abilities.

There is one final reason: space. Many gardeners just do not have enough of it. You have only a few square feet of space on your lawn, in a raised bed, or in containers on a patio, balcony, rooftop, or even doorstep. Summertime is tomato, pepper, and cucumber time. You don't have space to plant a second garden until you are finished with the first one. Do you really want to rip out your summer vegetables at the peak of their harvest to clear space for cauliflower and beets? Probably not, which is another reason to wait as long as possible, perhaps delaying a fall garden planting until August or September instead of July. If you have a small garden and need to make this decision, you might consider some faster maturing veggies (such as spinach or lettuce) over longer season choices (like broccoli or carrots).

You can extend your harvest season by using some of the methods mentioned later in this book. Oftentimes, even without an expensive greenhouse, you can cover and protect your crops easily. These coverings provide a few degrees of frost protection, keep off the wind and snow, and often allow your plants to make it all the way to a November, or even December or January harvest. Here is a picture of some homemade cold frames (from old window frames) being used to warm up the plants in a raised bed.

Chapter 5: Preparing the Soil and Fertilizing

Soil Preparation

Good garden soil contains a mixture of different ingredients. These include disintegrated fragments of rocks from the earth's crust, including sand, silt, and clay. Organic matter, which is formerly living plant tissue, is an important part of good soil as well. Soil provides structural support for a plant's roots and minerals for its nutrition (which usually should be supplemented by adding organic fertilizer as plant food as well). Whether you are planning to start your garden in ground rows, raised beds, or containers, it is important to give your plants healthy garden soil.

When growing plants directly in the ground, it is important to know what kind of soil you have already. You may be blessed with deep, rich growing soil and not need any amendment, but most soil can be improved by adding organic matter. If your soil is very heavy in clay, it may retain too much water, which can hurt your plants. If your soil has a high proportion of sand, then it may drain too quickly. The best way to remedy both types of soil is to dig in plenty of organic matter. Compost, aged manure, leaves, herbicide free lawn clippings, peat moss, and untreated sawdust are all examples of organic matter which can help improve soil structure. Place a thick layer of organic matter on top of your soil and dig it in as deeply as possible, so that plants' roots have at least 10-12 inches of rich, loose growing soil.

If you are gardening with raised beds or containers, you probably will need additional soil to fill them. You can purchase readymade potting soil, which is a good option for container growers who may not have much space to fill. However, this can get expensive if you are filling large containers or raised beds. Another option is to fill them partly with any compost you can make or obtain for free. To fill raised beds or containers, you can use almost any combination of soil and compost as well as other ingredients like peat, sand, and low grade manure. The most cost effective mix that works well in raised beds is about 25% sand or perlite, 25-50% compost, and 25-50% peat moss. All of these materials are available at your local nursery, landscape supply, or big box home improvement store.

Fertilizer

Your plants will need additional minerals also. Most garden soil is adequate for growing weeds, but does not have the mineralization needed to produce big, nutritious vegetable plants. Look for a bag or box of organic fertilizer at your local nursery. It should be a balanced organic fertilizer with measurable quantities of the three major nutrients that plants need to grow: Nitrogen (N), Phosphorus or Phosphate (P), and Potassium or Potash (K). Fertilizer bags and boxes are labeled with the three N-P-K numbers to indicate the available proportions of these three key nutrients. A balanced fertilizer should be somewhere in the range of 5-5-5, 4-6-3, 7-4-2, give or take a bit. Look for an "organic vegetable" or "organic garden" fertilizer, which contains whole foods that feed the plants and build the soil rather than the harsh synthetic, chemical derived ingredients found in conventional fertilizers. Most of them also feed the plants with micronutrients and trace minerals, including calcium, magnesium, iron, and sulfur, while some fertilizers include beneficial soil building bacteria.

Many cold season vegetables are heavy feeders which need lots of this plant food. In particular, plants producing a lot of green, leafy growth need lots of available nitrogen. Broccoli, cabbage, lettuce, and spinach, for example, probably need a fertilizer with a Nitrogen (the first N-P-K) number of "5" or higher.

Root and tuber vegetables such as carrots and potatoes need plenty of phosphorus and some potassium as well, so make sure that the second and third N-P-K numbers are no lower than "2" or "3". If you are growing only root vegetables, then even a "bulb and bloom" type fertilizer should work, provided that it has at least a little nitrogen. Fruiting vegetables are not well represented on our cool season list, because most vegetables that produce fruit or seeds (such as tomatoes, peppers, squash, cucumbers, and beans) need the heat and light energy of summertime. Aside from peas, broccoli, and cauliflower, all of the plants on our cool season list are grown for their edible leaves, stems, and roots, which require less light energy for plants to produce.

Fertilizers are available in sizes ranging from 3-5 pound boxes all the way up to 25 and 50 pound bags. For a small garden, a little goes a long way. Follow directions on the fertilizer package label to apply it in your garden. Generally, this consists of putting a spoonful or two next to each plant (but not touching it), scratching this into the top few inches of the soil, and watering this in well.

Chapter 6: Garden Rows, Raised Beds, and Containers

Garden Rows

Garden rows are the cheapest way to get started with a vegetable garden. While they are not as productive as raised beds, they do not require any additional building materials or as much extra soil. If you are starting a garden in a part of the yard that has never been used to make beds before, then you will need to dig up the soil and prepare it.

First, if there are any grass or weed plants growing on it, mow these as close as possible to the ground, leaving the trimmings in place. Mark off the area you want to use for your beds. The width of each bed should be from 1-3.5 feet, and they can be as long as you want to fit your space. Wide rows are more productive, since you are preparing a larger growing area with rich soil for plants. But make sure your beds are not too wide that you cannot reach the very middle of the bed to plant, fertilize, weed, tend, or harvest the center. Use chalk, string, or corner stakes to mark the bed location to dig.

After marking the space, use a shovel or spade to dig up a shovelful of soil that is 6-12 inches deep. You can turn this over so that any grass or weeds goes to the bottom. Using the shovel or spade, break up the soil as well as you can. If your soil is light and easy to work with, then you are lucky.

If your soil has a lot of sand or clay in it, then you will need to work in some organic matter, such as compost, manure, leaves, peat, or grass clippings. If it has lots of rocks or is pure clay, then you may want to consider investing in some containers or building your garden upwards (with a raised bed) rather than downwards. Keep digging up chunks, turning them over, and breaking them up until your whole bed area has been dug up and loosened.

Next, cover this soil with an inch or two of good compost, manure, or other organic matter. If you have enough organic matter for two or three inches of coverage, then use it all. Carefully dig this in to the top of the upturned soil, making sure not to bring up much grass or weeds, which will have a harder time regrowing if they are face down under the soil. Once you are done digging in the organic matter, water down the bed thoroughly, which will help the soil settle in.

Raised Beds

If you have the option to use raised beds, I believe they are the best growing option for most vegetables. These are beds where the soil is improved and mounded up above the ground level, usually requiring some walls to hold it up. Raised bed walls can be built from any materials available, including wood, stones, bricks, cinderblocks, tires, plastic, or metal.

While raised beds can be any size, shape, and height, building them at least 10-12 inches high ensures that plants will have plenty of growing room below. This is especially important when raised beds are built on top of concrete or really poor soil. In these situations, the raised bed essentially acts like a large container for plants to grow in. If you have good growing soil below, then a raised bed height of six inches or so will still enhance your vegetable production.

There are many advantages to using raised beds. First, the soil stays lighter and less compacted than ground soil, providing the plants' roots with plenty of spaces where air and water can reach them. This loose soil also drains well. Second, raised beds provide deeper, higher quality growing soil than exists in underground in most gardens. And third, the soil warms up more quickly in raised beds than the ground soil does, speeding plant growth. For all of these reasons, plants are more productive in raised beds than just about anywhere else (except for certain plants that grow particularly well in certain containers).

Additionally, raised beds simplify the tasks of gardening. People who are elderly, disabled, or have back problems will have an easier time accessing raised beds to tend, weed, and harvest from them. If you have birds eating your crops, you can cover raised beds with netting much more easily than you can cover crops on the ground. If your lettuce needs some protection from the hot summer sun in late summer, you can put in some shade cloth very easily. You can easily install a row cover to protect against pests or a protective greenhouse/cold frame covering to extend the season a bit longer.

Your gardening life is easier with raised beds, but it often requires some startup cash to buy the materials and get them built. For my raised beds, I used redwood lumber, which is naturally rot resistant. I built seven four by four foot (4'x4') raised beds to height of 20-24 inches each. I use four by four inch (4"x4") or thinner corner posts, building the sides from flat pieces of two by eight (2"x8") or two by ten (2"x10") lumber, secured with weather resistant screws. For one of the beds, which was built on top of a patio surface, I lined the inside with plastic sheeting to hold in the soil, secured to the wood siding inside by heavy duty staples. I lined the other beds with poultry wire at the bottom and stapled this in to prevent gophers from entering the beds underneath.

At the time, it cost me about $500 in materials and soil ingredients to fill the beds. Labor was free, since I learned to build them myself, eventually being able to build a whole bed in an eight hour day. You may be able to do better than I did in terms of cost, particularly if you can salvage some materials like old wood that someone is removing when replacing a fence or remodeling a house. Bricks and cinderblocks sometimes can be obtained for free, and can make a great permanent bed when they are mortared in.

Here is a picture of one of my beds, which is growing potatoes, broccoli, and blueberries. As you can see, part of the bed is connected to a chicken run. Our egg laying hens are kept away from the berries and vegetables by means of a temporary dog fence, which is attached to the chicken coop and run, and which gets moved around the garden periodically. While the chickens are using one bed, they fertilize, de-bug, and aerate the soil, preparing it for a later planting, and then move on to do the same thing in another location.

Chickens are very helpful in the garden, eating our kitchen scraps and providing plenty of fertilizer for the plants. If you would like to learn more about how to raise chickens for eggs in an urban backyard, please take a look at my e-book on this subject (available on Amazon), entitled *Backyard Chickens for Beginners*. Chickens are a lot easier to care for than most pets and you get fresh, organic eggs every day.

Containers

Many people do not have access to ground space for gardening. Some who do have ground space find that it is too rocky to plant or happens to be located almost entirely in the shade of a nearby tree or building. Perhaps you have a small yard that is covered over with a concrete or stone patio. No problem. Even if you do not want to build a raised bed on your patio, you can grow a garden in containers.

Every vegetable on our cool season list will grow just fine in containers. The key is to give them large enough containers to fit their root systems, provide them with fertilizer (since they cannot get any minerals form the ground), and keep them well watered. In many cases, you can get more production out of vegetables grown in containers than you can from them in the ground.

The size and depth of containers is important. In general, I would not plant vegetables in any container that is less than 12 inches wide at the top and less than 8 inches deep. The width is important in terms of how many plants you can fit in a container. If you follow the row spacing guidelines for each plant in Chapter 2, that should give plants enough space to grow without crowding one another. If you have deep containers, then you can get by with tighter spacing than this.

That depth is adequate for shallow rooted plants like peas and lettuce, but deeper rooted plants like carrots and broccoli will need 12 good inches of depth. Container growing will stunt some vegetable plants' growth a bit and you want to give the deep rooted plants as much growing space for their roots as possible. Yet there probably is no vegetable plant, even giant cabbage or indeterminate tomato, that cannot have a healthy life and produce effectively in a depth of 12 inches.

Take a look at the diagrams of root development that follow. I apologize in advance for the blurry quality, but they were created in 1927 when graphics were somewhat lower tech than today. I took them from a wonderful book called *Root Development of Vegetable Crops* by John E. Weaver and William E. Bruner (McGraw Hill 1927). You can read it online for free at the Soil and Health Library, along with many other out of print and public domain titles (http://www.soilandhealth.org).

Each square in a diagram represents one square foot underground. The first image below shows the roots of a lettuce plant at the age when you would first harvest its leaves. Besides the taproot, which mainly is searching for water, notice that all the growth is in the top few inches of soil. You could grow lettuce in a container with less than six inches of soil depth, probably even less for baby leaf lettuce. The same is true for peas, which are shallow rooted. And of course a smaller plant like mache could grow in almost any soil depth.

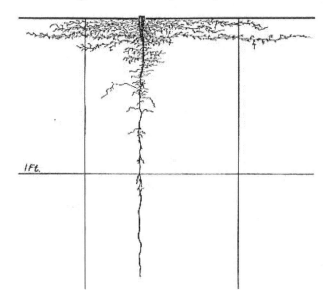

The second image shows a deeper rooted plant, cauliflower. Notice the grid squares are smaller, since we are looking at a larger area: these roots extend to a depth and width of five feet each. Cauliflower, like broccoli, cabbage, collards, and kale, needs plenty of growing space. This is not a lettuce plant where you can still pick some tender leaves and enjoy them if the plant is stunted and does not make it all the way to its full height potential. This is cauliflower, which will not produce its edible flowering heads until it is large and happy.

Don't try growing this puppy in a four inch deep dish. On the other hand, where is the vast bulk of its roots? Beyond that first square, we have a lot of secondary roots searching for nutrients and water. If you grew this plant in a container with a depth and width of 12-14 inches, providing it with fertile soil and plenty of water, you should get some large cauliflower heads. It will not have the same space to grow as it has in this picture, but it can get its business done in that much soil.

I know because I have grown broccoli, cauliflower, and kale before in just 12 inches of soil depth. The plants grew tall and produced plenty of food, apparently just as happy there as if they had been in the soil. Of course, when you try to take them out at the end of the season, the entire soil mass of the container is locked up in their root system. But that is a good problem to have, because it probably means you had a great harvest.

When I see a root mass like that at the end of the season, I usually just chop it up with a shovel and dump it into the compost (cole crop stems and roots can be pretty tough; another source once recommended beating them with a mallet before adding them to a compost pile or bin). Another option I have is to put this root mass in the chicken run, where our hens do a pretty quick job of scratching, pecking, and dismantling it as they look for grubs and worms. Sooner or later, the rest of that soil will end up back in the garden once it has been manured by chickens and/or composted.

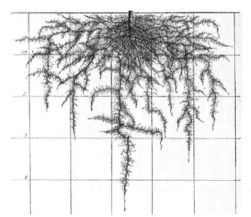

Cauliflower roots (each square is one square foot)

There are many different kinds of containers you can use to plant and grow your vegetables. For the vegetables in this book, I recommend four different kinds, each one of them ideally suited for a particular type of crop. However, these are by no means the only choices. Everything on our list will grow in just about any container, provided there is enough soil for the roots.

Four Recommended Container Types

Type 1: Self Watering Planter (for all vegetables, except root veggies and baby greens)

When self watering planters were fairly new, I raved about them in my first book, *Fresh Food From Small Spaces*. Now, every nursery and garden center seems to sell them, which I am glad to see. Everything from tomatoes to broccoli to chard seems to perform very, very well in this type of container.

A self watering planter is a container with a water reservoir. The water is soaked up slowly into the soil by the plants' roots, which take what they need. The plants form a two level root system, one level going down to the water and the other roots taking in plant food from the fertilizer that you mix into the first few inches of topsoil. There is lots of aeration for the roots and you can never overwater them, because you are filling up the water reservoir through a tube, not directly watering the soil or plants.

Almost everything grown in these self watering planters is tremendously successful. I would not hesitate to use them for any vegetable on our list. However, I do not think they are the best choice for either root (and tuber) crops or baby salad greens. They're not deep enough for full sized carrots, beets, potatoes, or turnips. And since the water comes from the bottom up, the top of the soil is too dry to grow baby leaf lettuce or other shallow rooted greens that are picked early.

The best known self watering planters are the Earthbox (available at www.earthbox.com) and the Tomato Success Kit from Gardeners Supply Company (available at www.gardeners.com). The latter has a full range of self watering planters in various sizes, but most of them are too small to grow vegetables. The planter box they use for their Tomato Success Kit is about the same size as the Earthbox (which is 29" L x 13.5" W x 11" H) and holds a similar volume of soil, around 1.5-2 cubic feet. Any self watering planter of this size or larger should make an excellent investment for your vegetable garden.

You could grow three good sized broccoli, cauliflower, or cabbage plants in one of these. Given the limited soil depth, they tend to be a little stunted and do not produce as well as they do in raised beds, but they will produce. Head lettuce, spinach, chard, parsley, or any of the other full sized leafy greens on our list will perform even better in a self watering planter of this size.

One caveat: shallow planted seeds do not germinate well in these planter boxes. The reason is that the water is soaked up from below, so the top of the soil remains dry. So for something like lettuce or carrots, which have very small seeds that are planted at 1/4 inch deep, that top 1/4 inch cannot stay wet enough to ensure their germination. It is best to start lettuce seeds somewhere else and transplant them. Baby lettuce and greens are not worth transporting; just grow them someplace else, as any regular pot or container will work fine.

For carrots and other root vegetables, you are better off growing them in a regular container that has a little more space. However, if a self watering planter is all you have, it will grow you some carrots. At the end of the carrot section, back in Chapter 2, you can see a picture showing the results of my carrot test with an Earthbox. We had to pick them a little earlier and did not get as many as we would have from a regular container, but it was not a bad little harvest of very tasty carrots.

Type 2: Deep Box or Tub (for root vegetables)

A carrot root can reach 10 inches long by itself, not even counting those stringy roots and hairs. It is possible to plant smaller varieties of carrots or pick them earlier as baby carrots, but full sized carrots need plenty of space. In fact, all root vegetables will benefit from deep soil, which also helps ensure that they will grow straight down rather than curling or branching out.

Therefore, use a deep container with at least 12 inches of soil depth for growing carrots, beets, turnips, Hamburg parsley root, and any other root vegetables. Potatoes, though not a root vegetable, grow underground and need deep soil to produce tubers. Small salad radishes might be the exception, because they are picked so early and are shallow rooted at that point, but longer radishes should be grown in deep containers as well.

The deep box or tub is any deep container. After I built my raised beds, I had enough scrap lumber laying around to build two very small planter boxes for the patio. Each one is about two feet by four feet (2'x4') and they are 12 inches tall. Those wooden boxes, assuming I remember to water them, are a great place for growing carrots.

Here are two other tub suggestions. First, one of those galvanized metal tubs they sell at nurseries and hardware stores should work pretty well. Those are plenty deep, and the last time I checked the price, I was surprised to see they were cheaper than some of the plastic containers. Second, any plastic Sterilite or Rubbermaid storage bin works great; I believe the 18 gallon bins are about 16 inches deep. With any bin or tub, you will need to punch some holes in the bottom to ensure proper drainage. Plants do not like getting wet feet, which is one reason so many home gardeners kill their houseplants.

Type 3: Shallow Box (for baby leaf lettuce and other baby greens)

If you plan to harvest lettuce at the baby leaf stage, then you do not need deep soil. The same is true for any other greens you grow for a baby leaf harvest, including arugula, chard, and kale. Honestly, you can pick any of these as early as you want. When they first germinate, they are known as sprouts, and many people grow sprouts in their kitchen even without soil. After about ten days, sprouts are classified as microgreens, which are often used in salads and garnishes at gourmet restaurants.

Two inches of soil depth would be adequate to grow either sprouts or microgreens. I recommend using a deep nursery seedling tray or slicing a milk carton in half lengthwise and filling each half with soil. Seeds for microgreens can even be placed on top of the soil, without a covering of soil, as long as you keep them wet for germination (keep a spray bottle nearby and squirt them whenever you walk past). Remember to lay the seeds thickly, since the plants will not grow out very much before you clip them.

Further along, baby leaf lettuce is harvested in around 28-35 days. By that time, the plant has grown some stronger roots (see the picture of lettuce roots in the last section), so you would need to be growing these plants in a soil depth of at least 6-8 inches. But the truth is that some gardeners are eating lettuce at every stage from seeding: sprouts, microgreens, and 2-3 week "baby lettuce" in addition to the more traditional 28-35 day baby leaf harvest. Just choose a container with enough depth to support your plants up until the time you need them.

Type 4: Fabric Pot or Plastic Growing Bag (for potatoes)

As I wrote in my book, *How to Grow Potatoes*, potatoes can produce a huge amount of spuds from fabric pots and plastic grow bags. In fact, you can grow more spuds in these soft sided containers than you can in the same amount of space in a raised bed, ground row, or any kind of container I know (without using some serious vertical growing tricks, as I explain in that book). The fabric pots are made from a cloth resembling felt and shaped into round, cylindrical containers. The plastic growing bags are like very deep shopping bags, sometimes made with handles for handing or carrying. These pots and bags are remarkably well suited for growing spuds.

There are several reasons they work so well. First, there are tiny air holes on the sides. When the roots hit air, they stop, branch out, and form more roots in new directions. More roots make more potatoes. Second, grow bags and fabric pots are usually dark in color, which absorbs solar heat and accelerates potato plant growth in cool seasons. But the air holes on the sides allow the soil to breath. This prevents them from overheating easily. Finally, all this air movement seems to really benefit potato plants, which like loose, well aerated soil.

The end result is that potatoes grow really, really well in these soft sided containers, so well that I recommend them above any other method…even above raised beds. Potatoes are the only plant I recommend growing in something other than a raised bed, since normally I consider raised beds to provide the best possible productivity for every vegetable. You can grow a ton of potatoes in raised beds, or in any garden row or deep container, but I doubt that you will exceed the growth possible in fabric pots and grow bags. Not without some serious tricks.

Chapter 7: Extending Your Season

By covering and protecting your vegetable plants, you can extend your growing season by several weeks or more. For gardeners in cold climates, this means a later harvest in early winter, an earlier start to the spring, and some fresh food from storage in between. Mild climate gardeners can use these techniques to grow food all through the coldest parts of the year. I will cover five of these techniques here: greenhouses, cold frames, hot beds, growing tunnels, and moving potted plants indoors. The first one can be quite expensive, the last one is free, and the others fall somewhere in between in terms of cost. Greenhouses and hot beds can be heated, which allows anyone to grow food anytime.

Hardiness of Vegetables at Low Temperatures

I am always skeptical about minimum temperatures for vegetables, not because the sources are untrustworthy, but because there are so many variables. For example, even when air temperatures are low, soil temperatures may remain slightly warmer, which can have a big effect on plants. One advantage of covering and protecting plants is that the daytime temperature increases can keep the soil temperatures a bit higher, even when night air is cold. Another advantage is that coverings can block the wind, which is the equivalent of a few extra degrees in warmth

Here are the accepted minimum temperatures that each of the following vegetables can withstand. If you can keep your plants a few degrees warmer with a covering, you will continue to have fresh vegetables available for as long as you can protect them. Remember that plant seeds will not germinate at these temperatures and plants will not grow well; these are minimum survival temperatures and they are approximate only. Degrees are listed in Fahrenheit.

Arugula: 15 degrees
Beets: 20 degrees

Bok Choy: 24 degrees
Broccoli/Cauliflower: 10-20 degrees
Cabbage: 5-10 degrees
Carrots: 15 degrees
Chard: 20 degrees
Chicory/Endive: 10 degrees
Collards: 20-24 degrees
Kale: 10 degrees
Kohlrabi: 10 degrees
Lettuce: 15-20 degrees (some varieties)
Mache: 10 degrees
Miners Lettuce: 10 degrees
Orach: unknown; similar to spinach and chard
Parsley: 10-20 degrees
Peas: 25-32 degrees
Potatoes: 32 degrees
Radishes: 10 degrees for long radishes; small ones freeze more easily
Scallions: 10-20 degrees
Spinach: 10-20 degrees
Tatsoi: 15-22 degrees
Turnips: 10 degrees
Upland Cress: 10-25 degrees

Greenhouses

A greenhouse is a solid framed structure, covered with a clear glazing such as glass, polycarbonate, or plastic. Higher temperatures and greater humidity can be maintained inside, speeding the growth of plants and enabling a gardener to grow crops that would not be possible outside. Greenhouses come in many designs and in sizes ranging from tiny patio greenhouses to large professional grower greenhouses. While even the small ones can be quite expensive to buy, it is possible to make your own greenhouse and save some money. Please see the Resources section below for more information on building your own greenhouse.

When buying or building a greenhouse, there are several important considerations. The first consideration is affordability versus quality. The most expensive greenhouses use strong, long lasting materials, such as steel support frames and UV-treated polycarbonate glazing, built for longevity and durability. Many homemade greenhouses use wood frames and glass windows, which are durable also. The cheapest greenhouses are made from plastic support frames and low end glazing, such as polyethylene film or fiberglass panels.

If you want a good greenhouse, it will cost you. A well built greenhouse made from high quality materials can be used for many years, probably paying for itself over that time due to its increased yields. However, paying several thousand dollars up front is not an option for many people, who are forced to look for cheaper greenhouses. Unfortunately, the cheaper ones do not stand the test of time, some of them having an effective life of no more than three years. If you plan to use your greenhouse for at least a few years, it is probably worthwhile to invest in a better one. Alternatively, you can look at some of the other options for covering your crops, such as cold frames, which can be a lot cheaper. This site has an extensive selection of smaller sized greenhouses (http://www.littlegreenhouse.com).

The next important consideration is whether or not to heat your greenhouse. In the wintertime, an unheated greenhouse provides a few extra degrees of warmth, helping to overcome cold spells and extend the season. However, while daytime temperatures get much warmer inside a greenhouse, nighttime temperatures can fall pretty low. This is not a problem in most climates, where winter hardy staples like lettuce, kale, mache, and scallions will keep on trucking when they're protected from the winds and snow.

In the coldest climates, you need a little more help to continue growing throughout the winter. Heating the greenhouse at night, usually by means of an electric cable, can maintain higher nighttime temperatures that allow many different plants to thrive. Keep in mind that you cannot trick them completely by heating, since day lengths are much shorter in the winter and this means less light energy for the plants. But in a heated greenhouse, you can grow a lot of crops, a lot faster, than you could without one. With a heated greenhouse, you need to be extra careful that the structure is sealed well and does not allow valuable heat to escape at night.

During the daytime, though, you will need a vent or fan. A vent lets heat escape through the top to prevent overheating, which can occur quickly on sunny days. Greenhouses that are prefabricated or come from a kit should have a vent already included in the design. If you are building your own, you can incorporate either a vent or an exhaust fan. Automatic vents, which you can buy online (Amazon sells several), either begin opening at a certain temperature like 72F or else they allow thermostatic control.

The Resources section at the end of this book contains links to additional information, including greenhouse building plans. In addition, it includes links to several websites that sell greenhouses at every level of the price spectrum. Here is a picture of a greenhouse in the United Kingdom with "windows" made from plastic soft drink bottles.

Growing Tunnels (Hoophouses)

The idea behind a growing tunnel or hoophouse is to use more affordable materials to achieve a greenhouse effect. This is really just a different version of a greenhouse. A growing tunnel can be as small as a cold frame or as large as a commercial greenhouse. Rather than building a full support structure, lengths of wire or plastic PVC pipe can be bent into half circle arches and placed every few feet, secured to the ground on each side of the bed. Steel pipes can also be bent into half circles and used. Plastic film is then stretched over the outside of this "frame" and fixed in place to create an enclosed greenhouse on the cheap.

These growing tunnels have become very popular in commercial agriculture. Here is a picture from the U.S.D.A. showing some Alabama farmers who are growing tomatoes in winter in a large tunnel.

Cold Frames

A cold frame is an open bottomed box with a clear framed lid that lets in sunlight. The walls are usually made of wood and often insulated, while the lid can be made of glass, plexiglass, polycarbonate, or any material that lets in light. Old window frames are often used as lids, also known as sashes, and hinged at the top to allow opening.

Because cold frames are used primarily in cool seasons, when the sun comes in at an angle (from the south, in the northern hemisphere), the top is slanted from back to front. In addition, soil can be mounded up on each side to provide additional insulation. And you can use any other type of insulation inside or outside the walls.

Some people also include a very simple passive solar heater inside. The most common method for this is to put a water filled container or two in your cold frames (preferably with each container painted black). The water heats up in the sunlight and then continues to heat the cold frame as temperatures drop. Water is very dense and releases a tremendous amount of energy as it cools, keeping your plants warmer at night.

Hotbeds

A hotbed is a cold frame that is supplied with extra heat. To provide extra heat, people normally use electric heating cables, but you can also keep the temperature up by using a light bulb, hot water pipes, or a thick layer of actively decomposing manure. A free article which describes how to build a cold frame and incorporate the hot manure layer is available on the Mother Earth News site at http://www.motherearthnews.com; just type "hot bed" into that site's search engine and it should come up. This image shows you a diagram.

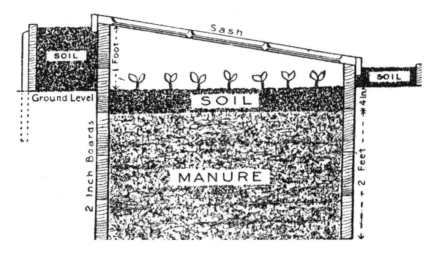

Electric soil heating cables are probably cheaper, more efficient, and safer than installing light bulbs. These cables are available at nurseries and online. Some cables have built in thermostats to maintain soil temperature in a moderate range. They are available in many different lengths, most commonly providing an output of 3.5-6.7 watts per foot. You generally need to use 1-2 feet of cable for each square foot of garden bed, and the cables are installed a few inches underground (follow installation directions that come with your cable). Do not cut the cables to achieve your desired length; just buy one with the approximate length to fit the size of your bed.

Here is a picture of a miniature growing tunnel (hoophouse) that doubles as a hotbed. The gardener has filled it with compost that is actively decomposing, helping to maintain a higher internal temperature.

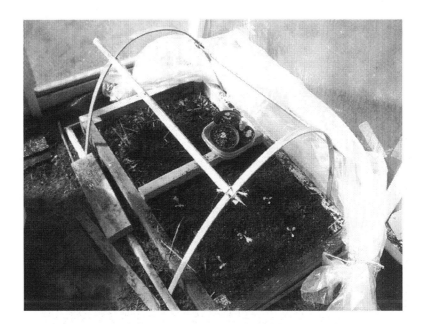

Moving Plants Indoors

If you grow vegetables in containers, there is always the possibility of moving these from a cold location to a warm one. Normally, this means bringing them indoors when the weather turns really cold. Obviously, this will not work for a bath tub sized planter box filled with hundreds of pounds of soil and potatoes, but how about a few smaller containers that each hold a parsley or spinach plant? Smaller containers with smaller plants can be brought indoors, where you can continue to clip a few leaves as you need them. Water the plants, keep them near a sunny window, and you should be able to keep them alive for a few extra weeks of fresh food in the wintertime.

Chapter 8: Harvesting and Storing Your Produce

Many vegetables can be stored for use during the winter months. Root vegetables and late maturing potatoes make the best storage candidates. Kohlrabi and cabbage can be kept for surprisingly long periods as well. Broccoli, cauliflower, peas, and all the leafy greens on our cold season list need to be used more quickly, generally within a week or two. However, any vegetables can be preserved by freezing them, while some can be pickled, canned, or dried as well.

While it is possible to store vegetables for long periods in the refrigerator, this tends to dry them out. Late maturing potatoes, beets, carrots, turnips, long types of radishes, cabbage, and kohlrabi will keep better in moist, cool conditions in a temperature range of 32-40 degrees F. A root cellar, unheated garage, basement, attic, or out building might be a good option, depending on what space you have available at your home. In times past, many people stored vegetables in storage clamps.

To make a clamp, select a dry part of your property. It can be a flat spot or a sloped area on the side of a hill. Dig a large hole there and line the bottom with a thick layer of straw (or shredded paper, sand, or sawdust from untreated wood). Place one layer of root vegetables on the straw, packed loosely to allow for air circulation. Cover this with another layer of the straw. Place another layer of root vegetables on top, cover it again, and repeat until you have filled most of the hole. Finally, cover it with a thick layer of straw on top and hold this down with some scrap wood or stones. Take out a few vegetables as you need to use them, starting on the top layer and working downward.

A storage clamp works best if you have a lot of produce to store for the winter. This method also leaves your food vulnerable to soil-based pests such as gophers, voles, or digging rats. You might be able to strengthen your clamp by lining it first with sharp gravel and then straw, then covering the top with a tough piece of wood that is drilled with small air holes and heavily weighted down with stones or cinderblocks. Another option is to take an old refrigerator or barrel and bury it most of the way in the hole, layering and covering as you would with an open clamp. On a smaller scale, you can just store vegetables in a cardboard box on a shelf in an unheated garage, cellar, or other cool location.

A company called Orka makes some cloth vegetable storage bags (you can find them on Amazon), which are very convenient. They work especially well for storing potatoes, onions, garlic, and root vegetables. They have handles for hanging, so if you have a storage area which is already pretty full, you will not need to use extra horizontal space. These could be hung from a wall or rafters.

Below is a list of the vegetables on our cool season list, which is sorted into different categories for storage purposes. After this information, we will cover storage by freezing, drying, pickling, and canning.

Root Vegetables, Potatoes, Cabbage, and Kohlrabi (store in moist, cool location, 32-40 degrees F)

Beets: Wash roots, trim tops to 1/2 inch, and store in perforated plastic bags for 3-4 months.

Carrots: Same directions as for beets.

Cabbage (heads): Cut off cabbage heads at the base when they are firm. Storage varieties can be kept in a plastic bag for up to three months in a cool place.

Cabbage (leafy, Chinese Cabbage): Same directions as above, but storage time is less, probably 1-2 months.

Kohlrabi: Cut off the root from the bottom and the leaf stems from the top. Kohlrabi will store in the refrigerator or another cool place for as long as 2-3 months.

Radishes: Wash and cut off tap root and top. Store small radishes for one month and longer radishes for 3-4 months.

Turnips: Wash roots, trim tops to 1/2 inch, and store in perforated plastic bags for up to 3-4 months.

Broccoli and Cauliflower (best kept in refrigerator)

Broccoli/Cauliflower: Does not store for long periods. In the refrigerator, fresh picked broccoli or cauliflower will last 1-2 weeks. It should be stored in a perforated plastic bag.

Leafy Greens (best kept in refrigerator)

Arugula, Chard, Chicory/Endive, Lettuce, Kale, Spinach, and other greens: To harvest, break off or cut leaf stems near the base. Store in plastic bags in the refrigerator for 1-3 weeks.

Others: Peas, Parsley, and Scallions

Peas: Sugar snap and snow peas can be washed and kept in a plastic bag in the refrigerator for up to two weeks. Shelled peas need to be frozen, since they will not last long otherwise.

Parsley: Pick the leaves and stems, wash, and keep in a plastic bag in the refrigerator for 1-2 weeks. Another way to extend your parsley season is to plant it in a pot you can move indoors. Keep harvesting parsley leaves as you need them, and you should get a few extra weeks out of it this way.

Scallions: Pick them when they get big enough to eat. Wash and cut off roots. Also cut off the tops of the stems. They will keep in a plastic bag in the refrigerator for two weeks. You can keep them longer and still use the white part at the base, but you will need to cut off the green leaves, which will wilt and decay.

Freezing Vegetables for Later Use

All vegetables on this list can be frozen. While it is possible to just wash, cut, and freeze your vegetables, it is best to blanch them first, which ensure that they will retain more flavor and color in the freezer. The basic procedure is this: Wash, trim, and chop potatoes or root vegetables into bite sized pieces. Prepare two pots of water, one filled with ice water and the other placed on the stove to boil.

You will also need a slotted spoon or pasta server for removing the vegetables from the hot water when they have been blanched. If you are only preparing one batch, then you can use a colander in the sink to strain the vegetables out of the water, but if you are blanching more than one batch at a time, then it seems wasteful to dump out your hot water each time, so a slotted spoon or pasta server works best for removing the vegetables from the water.

Once the vegetables have been chopped and the pot on the stove is boiling, dump them in and set a timer for exactly two minutes. As soon as two minutes are up, immediately remove the vegetables from the hot water and move them into the ice water. Once they are cooled, you can freeze them in plastic locking zipper bags or freezer containers for use at any time over the next year. These frozen vegetables will last at least 8-12 months.

Drying, Pickling, and Canning

There are several other ways to preserve your own vegetables: drying, canning, and pickling. In the Resources section at the end of this book, you will find the link for an excellent free guide to canning your own fresh vegetables. To pickle vegetables, you can use either a vinegar brine (like most pickled cucumbers you buy in the store) or lactic acid fermentation, which works for sauerkraut, kimchi, and other fermented vegetable dishes. My *Fresh Food From Small Spaces* book has some good sauerkraut and kimchi recipes. These recipes rely on natural yeasts and beneficial bacteria (like those in yogurt) for fermentation. If you would like a great free sauerkraut recipe and a stronger indoctrination into the world of Wild Fermentation, let me refer you to Sandor Katz's website at http://www.wildfermentation.com. For vinegar pickling and in depth canning information, I recommend the book *Putting Food By*, which is the definitive canning guide.

You can also dry vegetables to preserve them, and the Resources section at the end provides the link for a good free guide on this. Sun drying is possible, but probably not practical in cold weather. The other two methods are to use a food dehydrator machine or to dry them in the oven on the lowest temperature setting. Dried vegetables do not taste that good, but they can be added to soups or stews to reconstitute them. Root vegetables can be sliced, and will become dried vegetable chips, while leafy greens can be dried and turned into powder. If they are dried at low temperatures (under 108 degrees F), they will still have much of their nutrition intact.

Storing in Place

There is one final storage possibility. Carrots, beets, and other root vegetables can be stored in the ground. This only works well in climates where the ground is workable in wintertime, but which are cold enough so that the plants will not start growing again during the winter. After the plants freeze back in the late fall, cover the soil with a thick layer of mulch such as straw or leaves. Make sure this is kept in place with some wood, so that it does not blow away. Then whenever you need a few carrots or beets, just peel back the mulch and dig up a few roots to wash and eat. You can keep doing this into early spring, but make sure to pick and eat them all before they start growing again in early spring. It doesn't get much simpler than that!

My Secret Winter Nutrition

Finally, here is my secret to winter nutrition. I grow kale in a big raised bed until the plants start to get too old and tough. Picking all the leaves, I wash them (often enough to fill 3-4 paper shopping bags). I then turn on my juicer machine and juice all the leaves, which fill the juicer cup with dark green juice that is incredibly dense with vitamins, minerals, and antioxidants. (You can add a little of this to some other juice for an amazing nutritional boost, but this stuff is pretty hard to drink in any major amount.)

Then I fill up several ice cube trays with the kale juice. Once these are frozen, I empty them into a plastic locking zipper bag. Every time we make soup, stew, beans, eggs, pasta, you name it, I shave in a little kale ice. The kids never know what wonderful nutrition they are getting. I do this a couple of times per year and so we always have a steady supply.

Resources
Here are some great resources for further information. For the Kindle edition of this book, it is easy for me to keep the Internet links updated. For the print edition, if a link no longer works, you can try going to the main website that is listed and then searching for the product or article.

Cold Hardy Vegetables
Additional Information on Cold Hardy Vegetables from University of Minnesota and Oregon State University:
http://www.extension.umn.edu/distribution/horticulture/M1227.html
http://ir.library.oregonstate.edu/xmlui/bitstream/handle/1957/20754/pnw548.pdf?sequence=3

Vegetable Seed Suppliers (Online Ordering)

Johnny's Selected Seeds: http://www.johnnyseeds.com

Territorial Seed Company: http://www.territorialseed.com

Park Seed: http://parkseed.com

High Mowing Organic Seeds: http://www.highmowingseeds.com

Peaceful Valley Farm & Garden Supply: www.groworganic.com

Seed Potato Suppliers

Potato Garden: http://www.potatogarden.com

Irish Eyes Garden Seeds: http://irisheyesgardenseeds.com

Moose Tubers: http://www.fedcoseeds.com/moose.htm

Storing Vegetables
Information from Cornell and Iowa State Universities on How to Store Vegetables:

http://www.gardening.cornell.edu/factsheets/vegetables/storage.pdf

http://www.extension.iastate.edu/Publications/pm731.pdf

Canning Vegetables

Excellent free guide:
http://www.uri.edu/ce/ceec/food/documents/GH%201454.pdf

Drying Vegetables

Good free overview:
http://nchfp.uga.edu/publications/uga/uga_dry_fruit.pdf

Sauerkraut and Wild Fermentation

Sandor Katz's website: http://www.wildfermentation.com/making-sauerkraut-2

Building a Greenhouse

DIY Plans for 12'x14' greenhouse made primarily of PVC pipe and plastic sheeting:
http://www.bae.ncsu.edu/programs/extension/publicat/postharv/green/small_greenhouse.pdf

Links to Free Greenhouse Building Plans and Information:
http://www.sherrysgreenhouse.com/pages/structures/greenhouses-build.html

How to Build Your Own Greenhouse book: http://www.amazon.com/How-Build-Your-Own-Greenhouse/dp/158017647X/ref=sr_1_2?s=books&ie=UTF8&qid=1340396975&sr=1-2&keywords=building+greenhouse

Greenhouses for Sale Online

Good selection of smaller greenhouses: http://www.littlegreenhouse.com/flowerhouse.shtml

All sizes of greenhouses: http://www.4seasongreenhouse.com/

Building Cold Frames and Hot Beds

Excellent article from Mother Earth News:
http://www.motherearthnews.com/modern-homesteading/how-to-build-a-hotbed-zmaz76mazhar.aspx

Information from University of Missouri and Purdue Extension Programs:

In-Depth Book on Growing Vegetables in Unheated Greenhouses in Winter
Eliot Coleman is the master of growing vegetables in unheated greenhouses, which he does in the wintertime in Maine. He has several good books, which are available on Amazon.

My Publications

Author Info

R.J. Ruppenthal is a licensed attorney and college professor who has a passion for growing and raising some of his own food. He is based in California, though he has experience trying to grow winter vegetables in Wisconsin. He regularly writes and blogs about fruit and vegetable gardening, growing food in small urban spaces, sustainability, and raising backyard chickens. On occasion, he even pens something about law or government. You can follow his blogs at http://www.amazon.com/R.J.-Ruppenthal/e/B00852ZTT2/ref=ntt_athr_dp_pel_1

My Publications

1. *How to Grow Potatoes: Planting and Harvesting Organic Food From Your Patio, Rooftop, Balcony, or Backyard Garden*

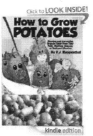

Description from Amazon:
Perfect beginners guide to growing potatoes. This booklet explains how to plant and grow organic potatoes for food in the home garden. Recommended for backyard gardeners and container gardeners with small city-sized yards, patios, balconies, decks, and rooftops.

- Why Grow Potatoes? Six Great Reasons
- Different Kinds of Potatoes (and Where to Get Them)
- Growing in Containers, Raised Beds, and Traditional Rows
- Planting and Hilling Potatoes
- Soil, Fertilizer, and Watering Needs
- Harvesting Potatoes
- Storing Potatoes for Later Use
- *Bonus*: Two Secret Tips for Getting More (and More Delicious) Potatoes

2. *How to Sprout Raw Food: Grow an Indoor Organic Garden with Wheatgrass, Bean Sprouts, Grain Sprouts, Microgreens, and More*

Description from Amazon:

Grow Your Own Raw Food Anywhere!

Would you like to grow some of your own food this year? Indoors? With no sunlight or soil? At any time of the year and at all times of the year? Sprouts allow you to do all that and more. In fact, you can grow all the vegetables your body needs (plus all the protein as well) in an area that's no bigger than your microwave oven. I grow sprouts on top of my refrigerator, harvesting baskets of fresh, raw food every week without even going outside.

Growing sprouts is simple and it's cheap. Sprouts can provide you with the power-packed nutrition your body needs at a fraction of the price of store bought food. You can save money while eating right. There's no dirt, no pests, and no weeding required.

Raw Food Salads, Sandwiches, Cereals, and More!

This short guide will teach you how to grow sprouts and enjoy eating them. If you like salads, I'll show you how to make delicious bowlfuls with tasty mild or spicy sprouts. If you enjoy eating cereal for breakfast, try some sprouted grains with natural malt sugars that nourish your body and taste far better than boxed cereals.

Need to lose a few pounds?

Simply eating a few more sprouted beans will keep you feeling fuller and eating fewer carbs. Toss some bean sprouts, lentil sprouts, or pea sprouts into your next rice or pasta dish; they make great burgers as well. You'll find that your body absorbs the protein better when the beans are sprouted, which usually reduces flatulence as well. All this nutrition, protein, and fiber will have you shedding a few pounds in a hurry.

Topics Include:

1. Superfood Sprouts
Cheap, Easy to Grow, Provide Year-Round Nutrition

2. The Benefits of Raw Food
Lose Weight, Nourish Your Body, and Stimulate Energy Levels

3. Sprouting Equipment and How to Use It
Trays, Jars, Bags, Automatic Sprouters, and Wheatgrass Juicers

4. Salad and Sandwich Sprouts
Alfalfa, Clover, Radish, and Broccoli

5. Bean Sprouts
Mung Beans, Soy Beans, Lentils, Peas, and More

6. Grain Sprouts
Wheat, Barley, Rye, Oats, Triticale, Quinoa, and Other Grains

7. Seed and Nut Sprouts
Sunflower, Sesame, Pumpkin, Peanut, and Flax

8. Seasoning Sprouts
Basil, Celery, Cress, Dill, Fenugreek, Mustard, Onion Family, and More

9. How to Grow Microgreens
Grow a Gourmet Baby Salad, Anytime, Anyplace!

10. Wheatgrass Juice From Homegrown Sprouts
How to Grow and Juice Your Own Wheatgrass

11. Where to Get the Best Sprouting Seeds
Trusted Sources for the Freshest Quality

12. Where to Find the Best Raw Food Sprout Recipes
Delicious ways to enjoy your sprouts, raw or cooked

3. *Backyard Chickens for Beginners: Getting the Best Chickens, Choosing Coops, Feeding and Care, and Beating City Chicken Laws*

Description from Amazon:
Excellent booklet for beginners on how to start a backyard mini-flock of 2-4 chickens and get fresh eggs every day. Written by the author of the best-selling Fresh Food From Small Spaces book, a former columnist for Urban Farm magazine. (Updated 2012 Version)

Topics include:
- Fresh Eggs Every Day
- How Much Space Do You Need?
- Building or Buying a Coop
- Feeders, Waterers, Nesting Boxes, and Roosts
- Getting Chicks or Chickens
- Feeding Your Chickens
- Tips for Cold Climates
- Health and Safety
- Dealing with Neighbors, City Chicken Laws, and Other Challenges
- Resources: Everything You Need!

4. *Blueberries in Your Backyard: How to Grow America's Hottest Antioxidant Fruit for Food, Health, and Extra Money*

Description from Amazon:
Perfect blueberry growing guide for beginners. This booklet explains how to plant and grow blueberries in the home garden. Recommended for backyard gardeners with small city-sized yards, patios, balconies, decks, and rooftops. (Updated 2012 version)

Topics include:
- Why Grow Blueberries? Six Great Reasons
- Blueberries for Every Climate (and where to get them)
- Grow Blueberries Almost Anywhere: Doorsteps, Patios, Balconies, Rooftops, and Yards
- Perfect Blueberry Soil (regular garden soil kills them, but they will thrive in this!)
- How to Plant and Grow Blueberries in Raised Beds and Containers
- Feeding, Watering, and Caring for Your Blueberry Bushes
- Making Extra Money Growing Blueberries

Photo credits: Cover images: CanStockphoto, www.canstockphoto.com
CSA veggies: Flickr user "aMichiganMom", www.flickr.com
Arugula: Flickr user "little blue hen", www.flickr.com
Broccoli: Flickr user "edibleoffice", www.flickr.com
Cabbage snow: Flickr user "quinn.anya", www.flickr.com
Kohlrabi: La Grande Farmers' Market
Mache: Flickr user "rfarmer", www.flickr.com
Window frames: Flickr user "dyogi", www.flickr.com
Potato grow bags: Courtesy of Gardeners Supply Company
Greenhouse of bottles: www.geograph.org.uk, NH5319
Large growing tunnel with farmers: http://blogs.usda.gov/tag/hoop-house
Miniature growing tunnel "Flickr user "greengardenvienna", www.flickr.com
Other photos: Rights held by author or public domain

53671132R00034

Made in the USA
San Bernardino, CA
24 September 2017